He Did What?

True Stories of the Absurd, Depraved, and Bizarrely Insightful

By Chris Santiago

ISBN: 978-0-578-88700-5

Dedication

To all who inspired or were the subjects of any of these stories, I offer my truest and most heartfelt thanks. As a dedi-
cation, this collection is dedicated to anyone who has ever
told me a great story.

Table of Contents

Preface

This isn't a "cop book."

It isn't a procedural, it isn't a true crime exposé, it isn't a whodunnit. Most "cop books" focus on those exact things. They're usually all based on true stories, detailing how the feds brought down the mafia, how detectives tracked the Zodiac Killer, or some variation thereof. We've all heard those stories, we've read them, we've watched them. Those stories are all fascinating pieces of work in their own right, but that's not what this book is about.

It's also not about the friendships or the life-long bonds that front line guys form while toughing it out. It's not about how guys with the warrior ethos would take a bullet for their partners. Yes, there are those emotionally based, duty bound elements to the job. Anyone who has ever raised their hand and sworn an oath will attest to that. But this isn't a recruiting piece, and it definitely doesn't sexy up the experience. This doesn't break down the car chases or the foot pursuits or the close calls. If you're expecting that, expect to be disappointed.

This isn't going to make the pitch that police work is unbelievably hard or try to emphasize how most cops have to make split second decisions, or how most cops are good guys and it's only a few bad apples that give them all a bad name. This isn't a piece of pro-law enforcement propaganda. Similarly, it also isn't a critique on the profession or a commentary on the institution of policing. If you're looking for that kind of commentary, look elsewhere, because you're not gonna find it here.

It's also not about the day-to-day struggle of working a patrol beat. This isn't a day in the life kind of book. Yes, the grind beats you down. Yes, navigating bureaucracies can be exhausting. Yes, it can be hard on relationships and your personal life. Sure, those elements do play into some of these stories, but that's just to set the stage, that's just the kicking off point. Everything needs at least a little context.

Because this isn't just a book of stories; it's a book about storytelling.

When I had about six years on the job, I worked with an old timer who told me about his dad, who happened to be another old, retired police officer. Back in the day, he had this partner who got in the habit of writing a small blurb in a journal after every shift. It would summarize what he did that day, and while he definitely noted the crazier stories, there were also entries that were just mundane. Not every shift involves a close brush with death. He did this for years, and by the time he retired, he had a whole collection of stories. He turned some of those stories into books and ultimately launched a very successful writing career.

It got me thinking that maybe I should do something similar. I'd had some pretty interesting experiences, so I started making a list of memorable cases, memorable moments. I poured through old reports to jog my memory. And even though they were all memorable, there was something missing from them, a unifying theme. I figured I'd start writing anyway.

The original intent of this was to simply serve as a collection of entertaining stories, written in a voice that was hopefully unique enough to keep a reader's attention. But as each story played out, I started to notice some common themes developing, and they weren't unique to police work. That's just the lens from which I started writing. And as I continued writing and dissecting each of those stories, they jogged other memories which sent me down other paths and away from where I originally started. By the time I finished, maybe only half of these stories even ended up being police related.

So while I do pull from my experiences working in law enforcement, this is by no means a "cop book." I do get into some procedural discussion to provide context for why certain things are happening, but that's not the focal point. The real point is the stories themselves.

By its nature, a big part of police work is asking people what happened, and it's through that prism of listening to other people's stories and then retelling them myself, that the real themes take form. Police work is simply unique in how it offers such a wide glimpse into the way different people experience the world. And it's through those stories that we glean certain truths that we otherwise may never have seen.

One of those truths? People are fucking *wild*.

Everything in this collection is true, save for some of the names and locations which I've changed in order to obscure some identities. A lot of these stories are gritty, embarrassing, shameful, and uncomfortable. That's the world, and to shy away from it would be to deny reality. And that is one thing that truthful storytelling does not do.

I've done what I can to give credit within the main pages themselves for the parts of this that were not my own. One story in particular I relay as it was told to me. It's a chapter within this book about a time I heard a story from someone else, so it's kind of a story within a story within a story. My buddy actually first featured it in a blog post, and it was so perfectly constructed and honest as to how he originally told me the story, I simply had to adapt it.

In order to stay as true to his telling as possible, I borrowed as much as I could from the original with only slight changes for consistency and voice. But in the grand scheme, it's all true. Thanks Josh.

Happy reading.

*   *   *

P.S. I guess this book is technically considered memoir, or maybe creative non-fiction. It's being told from my perspective and my perspective alone unless otherwise noted, and generally I'm relaying everything as best as I can remember. You know, from memory. Quotes are probably not verbatim, conversations not exact, you get the idea. Names, locations, all that other stuff has been altered to obscure identities and to protect the innocent as well as the guilty. So don't get all butt-hurt if something sounds a little too similar to your own tale, it's more than likely a coincidence. Related, this is in no way endorsed by any particular police department, military branch, school, or other group or organization which might get all cross-minded about showing up in a book. Nothing in it is classified or otherwise confidential. It's my book and it features my own thoughts on the subjects, philosophical or otherwise, so get on board with that or close it and go read something else. Good luck...

The Disappearing Thumb

I'll always have a strange relationship with the song "Tainted Love" by Soft Cell.

It's the perfect coda to what played out on a random day in downtown Los Angeles sometime around the summer of 2017. Now this story is entirely true. I'm a cop. At the time, I had about five years on the job and was working LAPD's Central Division. And within Central Division, I was specifically assigned to the Safer Cities Initiative Task Force, a specialized unit within the division that patrolled Skid Row, the homeless and drug capitol of America.

Skid Row is situated in downtown Los Angeles and spans an area which is known locally, at least among the police officers who patrol there, as "the box." The area is bound to the north by 4th St. and Little Tokyo, 7th St. to the south, Los Angeles St. to the west, and Alameda St. and the arts district to the east. While those are the official boundaries of the box, Skid Row actually extends a bit beyond those limits and gradually dies off, giving way to more "normal" areas the farther you get. Even with that, there are still pockets, or mini Skid Rows, scattered throughout the city. The presence of mini Skid Rows has ebbed and flowed over the years, but one place that's never actually changed is the box.

It's a modern-day wild west in all its lawlessness and chaos. If you've been there, or perhaps accidentally passed through, you know exactly what I'm talking about – it's worth noting that people accidentally pass through surprisingly often due to the one-way streets and the fact that the average Angelino can't seem to get their east and west directions figured out. At 550 west 7th St. you can rent a penthouse apartment for $15,000 a month, while at 550 east 7th St. you can get stabbed over a $20 crack rock.

Most of the streets are almost completely lined with tents. Most block the entire sidewalk, forcing pedestrians to walk in the street. The sidewalk areas which are not blocked directly by tents are lined with debris and personal items – furniture, trash cans, bicycles – almost anything you can think of really. Imagine what a Wal-Mart of homelessness would look like, or more accurately, what the inside of one those hoarder houses on TLC would look like, except, you know…outside.

Many of the tents go beyond just being tents. Entire structures are erected on the sidewalk and covered by tarps, which may be attached on one end to an adjacent building or gate. You can even find full on wooden building frames sitting square in the middle of the sidewalk, stretching from building to curb, upwards of twenty feet long and with the kind of woodworking and craftmanship you would see on most legitimate construction sites. Except instead of the wood structure being attached to an actual foundation, it's

just sitting on the sidewalk. It's a nightmare for local businesses and anyone with concerns as to fire safety, but again,
it's the wild west.

Inside those tents is a variety of findings spanning all
levels of poverty and luxury, madness and brilliance. Next
to one tent on the northwest corner of San Pedro St. and 7th
St, you can usually see a series of extension cords running
from an open electrical gang box on a nearby light pole into
the back corner of a large camping tent. Inside that tent,
somebody has absolutely decked it out with a fully powered
suite including a refrigerator, forty-inch television, video
game consoles, microwave, lava lamp, digital clock, audio
system, electric grill, and portable air conditioner. There's
even a lazy boy chair, a small folding table, a box spring with
mattress, and a fully made bed with pillows and blankets.
The owner of that tent lives in what I would call relative
street luxury, having rigged up a system, albeit hazardous,
that allows him to siphon free electricity from the city.
Surely a mark of technical expertise and innovation. He was
probably an electrician in his previous life before it got up-
ended by a combination of drugs, crime, and mental illness.
Illegal, incredibly unsafe, but brilliant in its own right. And
somehow, nobody bothers him.

Right next to his tent, another with a similar appearance
from the outside, minus the electrical cords. But on the inside, a dirty mattress with piles upon piles of soiled clothes
and blankets, all with a moist, musty stench mixed with the
scent of burning sage candles and half eaten food items. If
you look close enough, you can see the bed bugs and fleas
burrowed amidst the piles of clothes and blankets. Completely infested. Rats and roaches wandering freely in and

3

out the tent as if it was their own. And the human occupant, more a shell of a person than an actual living being. Too mentally far gone to care in the slightest, laying right smack in the middle of it. Just another local.

Next to that tent sits another looking just as unassuming as the other two, except this one has a combination lock on the flap. If you were to go inside, you would see two lawn chairs and a small folding table and nothing else. Nobody actually lives in this tent – most of the time nobody even frequents it. This is a dealer's tent. Most cops who've worked the area for some time will tell you maybe half the tents out there are usually vacant like this, or pretty close to it.

When we began hitting the local dealers with aggressive narcotics enforcement, they decided to move their operations inside the tents so they wouldn't be visible from the streets. The local ordinances and court orders didn't exactly help, because they specifically forbade officers from seizing the tents and classified them as full-on dwellings. In order to get inside a tent, you need a warrant. If a uniformed cop can't see the hand-to-hand transactions, it's a lot harder to put a dope case on somebody short of sending in an undercover posing as a junkie to conduct a buy. On most nights, like clockwork, after we finished our shifts and were headed home, we would drive past tents like these and see lines of people ten deep, waiting to get their fix. Eventually the dealers and junkies would catch on to when our shifts would change, wait for the lull, and then it was like Black Friday. It's a constant game of adjustment and adaptation, with somebody ultimately always being open for business.

Beyond the throngs of tents lining the streets you'd find the people. A whole host of characters milling about, disconnected yet somehow plugged into the greater energy of the area, causing this godforsaken part of the city to take on a personality of its own. Especially during the day, a bizarre ecosystem bristles with life. Local immigrant owned businesses like the flower and toy shops teem with people driving in from outside the area to get a deal. Corner market stores receive deliveries. Workers from all the mental health and service facilities wander to and from their buildings, out to lunch and back. Homeless outreach groups, church volunteers, and community organizers host small impromptu events in nearby San Julian and Gladys Parks. And among all these more normal elements, hundreds upon hundreds of people hanging outside their tents, bringing to life a neighborhood with its own distinct energy – drinking, playing cards, smoking, talking trash, picking fights, blasting music. And oddly enough it somehow brings a sense of order – structure without structure, a truly organic ecosystem.

And then there are the wanderers, those shuffling about aimlessly in zombie-like stupor, their brains scrambled from years of hard drug use and street-borne trauma, oftentimes blurring the lines of mental illness with drug induced delirium. Nine times out of ten, anybody you run into in the area suffers from some form of mental illness, with schizophrenia, bipolar disorder, and agitated delirium consisting of the most frequent of cases. Most sufferers self-medicate with hard drugs and alcohol, which doesn't exactly promote a stable environment.

Most interactions with this crowd are a second away from going south in a hurry, and the result is a tinderbox that begets a constant state of violent crime. Regardless of how crazy a person might be or what history they might have, regardless if their circumstances are beyond their control, a violent assault is a violent assault. It doesn't matter if they're schizophrenic or bipolar and suddenly snapped on someone who had been irritating them – which was probably due to that person's own inability to recognize warnings and social cues – but ultimately a hammer to the head is still a hammer to the head, a stabbing is still a stabbing, and knocking some-one unconscious is still knocking someone unconscious. They're all felony crimes and they land people in jail. When they get out, they have nowhere to go, so they venture back into this world, feeding the cycle of chaos and violence.

Then beyond these perpetually troubled individuals are the real bad guys, the true criminals. The gangsters and drug dealers who don't even live in the area, but live in other neighborhoods and come into Skid Row to sell. This crowd is usually very easy to spot because they look clean and dis-tinctly not homeless. And when you look a little closer, you can tell they're not crazy either. They're fully aware of their environment, calculating, operative. They are the real prob-lems, those few who would prey upon the weaknesses of the sufferers, feeding the beast. They enlist the help of local us-ers to insulate themselves from enforcement, and get these useful idiots caught up in the sales game. While no particular arrest is the same, you can learn to spot the patterns and identify who and how the different elements are involved.

Nestled in the middle of all of this is Central Station, home of the classic Adam-12. This police station, arguably one of the largest commands in the LAPD, is home to sev-eral different specialized units ranging from Central Traffic to Gang and Narcotics Division to SWAT (SWAT has since moved to a different building). Central is also home to one of the largest patrol deployments. A beacon of law and order, plopped right down in the middle of the most looney tunes place on earth. Homeless people camping out along the ramparts next to the flagpole, junkies shooting up on the stairs leading to the main entrance, and a lady so out of her mind she is squatted down in the planter, amidst the flowers and brambles, taking a shit in a Styrofoam to-go container while having a full-on conversation with herself.

Along Wall St. which runs north and south on the east side of the building is the vehicle entrance, one driveway in and one driveway out, which is the primary entrance for employees arriving and leaving in their personal vehicles as well as for police cars coming to and from the station. The entrance is manned by one officer in a small guard shack. It's the easiest assignment because he isn't expected to take reports; he just has to make sure people in personal or plain cars flash a badge or ID as they drive in, and to keep any errant Skid Row locals from wandering into the station. Next to the guard shack is a car wash that only works maybe fifteen percent of the time, and a large dumpster. Most days you can find a crazy person rifling through the trash while the officer in the guard shack reads a newspaper, numb to the regular shenanigans taking place before his very eyes.

*   *   *

I was working watch five, a mid-PM swing shift. My partner was a fairly petite but sharp girl I had known since our time in the academy, Gina. During the academy, I was the class leader – I fell into this role due to my previous military background – and she was the class guide – the class guide is usually the top athlete, or at least the best runner, and is responsible for carrying the guidon, a six foot flag pole with our class banner, displayed proudly during formation and platoon runs. During formation or drill, I was typically in front of or alongside the main platoon, doing everything from calling cadence to marching the class from location to location. She was usually right up front near me with the guidon, so essentially, we were the two most visible members of the class. Then when it came to partnering up for self-defense drills or tactics, we were usually partnered up just because of proximity, so we naturally became good friends.

After the academy, I went to Central for probation and she went to a valley division. We didn't run into each other for a couple years after that until I made my way back to Central following a short stint on the west side and she transferred to Central after working a narcotics assignment. Once she arrived at Central, I got her into my unit and we partnered up. It was a good fit. We already knew each other and we worked well together. The really great thing was that I liked chasing dope, and she had a narco background, so we were both often on the same page in terms of how we viewed police work. When you switch back and forth between partners, you never know who you will be working with or what they will be into. Some guys consider themselves elephant hunters – they go out and only want the big catch and will dodge anything they deem as small beans. Others like stopping cars or doing traffic enforcement, others like jamming up drinkers and gamblers, others like simply handling the radio. Gina and I liked drugs.

Gina was a good partner – smart, reliable, savvy, trustworthy. Funny thing about Gina is that unbeknownst to me, she always went by her middle name, Janet. As long as I had known her though, I always called her by her first name. It wasn't until one of her old supervisors came looking for her at our unit and was asking around for someone named Janet, and I had no idea who that was, that it was a surprise when I finally learned he was looking for her. The corollary to that is she didn't realize Santiago was my last name – she thought it was my first name. Apparently, my last name is most commonly a first name in all of Latin America except in Puerto Rico, and I had no idea. Odd how we had known each other that long and didn't even really know each other's names.

We developed a solid routine for mostly every shift. Luckily for us, our sergeant knew we liked to chase dope and if given the freedom to go hunting, we would usually bring in a good multi-arrest sales case or other solid caper every night. Immediately after roll call, we would check out a car and grab our gear from the kitroom, load up our vehicle, log onto the deployment system, and then make our way back into the office.

In the office was a suite of computers which resembled the kind of command center you might see in a movie. Each of the monitors was linked up to a camera which covered certain areas within Skid Row. Due to the nature of the area with the uniquely high levels of violent crime, the police department had installed cameras on light poles and buildings whose owners wanted to partner with us, all in the hopes that the cameras could be used as a tool to combat crime.

Because the cameras only covered what was publicly visible anyway, there was no need for any special warrants or permissions to use them. The cameras were a great tool to help identify suspects in violent crimes as well as piece together complicated narcotics sales schemes between multiple players. It was akin to having an officer with a set of binoculars posted up on rooftops or on corners to monitor the streets. It was no secret we had cameras everywhere – hell, dealers would post up right outside the police station anyway. As if a sense of consequence was actually a thing...

Our usual move was to check the cameras before even hitting the streets, simply to see who was out and about, and this night was no different. It would give us an idea of what the playground was like and maybe give us an insight into how we might plan the flow of the shift. After taking a look at the cameras, we decided on a game plan. We saw a few of our normal players, and activity seemed to be a bit busier than usual. At 5th and San Julian, we saw one guy who we had yet to identify, but we knew he was tied into the sales game as a main player. We would work on that for the night, see if we could find a way to identify him and build a case, or who knows, maybe stumble into something else. Neither of us had eaten, so we would start out the shift by grabbing some food, come back, and eat while we watched the cameras. That would give it a chance to get dark outside, which would allow us to scope out a rooftop we had been eyeing where we would have a solid vantage point to see what our guy was up to. Then we'd see what we would see and hopefully come back with some good results.

I'm driving that day, so Gina is working the radio and keeping the books. We drive out of the station garage and head south on Wall St. towards 6th. We pass through the intersection and we both notice a guy on the driver side trying to flag us down.

Damn, already? We can't even eat without getting roped into something. Straight nonsense...

I slow the car and pull up to the guy. He's a black guy, about six-foot tall, average weight, doesn't particularly stand out as a gangster or crazy person, maybe he just works at the shelter nearby as a volunteer.

"Hey, what's up?" I ask.

Pointing, "Officers, you guys gotta do something about this dude down there, I've been trying to flag one of you guys down for the last half hour."

"Why don't you just make a radio call?"

"Naa, I don't call the po-lice!"

Obviously not as sensible a guy as I had hoped.

I ask, "Who is it? What's he doing?"

Still pointing, "He's had his pants off, going around buck ass naked, whackin' off, it's fucked up, we can't be having people doing that shit around here, you gotta at least tell him to stop."

He motions behind us towards where we just drove past maybe thirty yards back on the passenger side. I look in the rearview mirror and Gina turns in her seat. We both see a man with a medium complexion, maybe about five foot eight, wearing no shirt, no shoes, and pulling *on* a pair of jeans. That has to be him.

I say, "Ok give us a sec, we'll go talk to him."

I put the car in reverse and back up towards the guy. Gina calls out from the car. "Hey, are you the one who's out here masturbating?"

That's a real question police officers have to ask.

"Why are people telling us you're out here masturbating where everyone can see?"

"Oh, I don't know, I wasn't doing anything, I don't know – the guy continues to stammer awkwardly so I chime in.

"Don't tell us it wasn't you, they pointed you out directly and you're not even wearing pants. You're pulling them on so they were obviously off before."

"Oh, I don't know, I'm ok."

"We don't want to get calls anymore of you jacking off out here, do that inside somewhere, don't be nasty."

"Ok ok, thank you, thank you."

I ask him, out of due diligence and almost a force of habit, "Are you on parole or probation?"

"I'm on parole."

"You been checking in?"

"Yeah yeah, I just checked in today."

"Oh really? Alright, we're gonna do a quick check on you, then get you out of here, ok?"

"Alright, no problem."

He knows the rules, this isn't his first rodeo. Anyone on parole or probation is required per the conditions of their release to comply with impromptu compliance checks and must submit to search and seizure for any reason by law enforcement.

Gina goes over the radio to broadcast our location. "1FB24, show us code six on Wall south of 6th on one." The RTO (radio transmission operator) repeats her broadcast and updates our status. This is all standard, nothing unusual. Whenever a unit conducts some kind of activity, whether it be a traffic stop, a ped stop, walking a foot beat, or arriving at a crime scene, they will "go code six" so in the event of an emergency, responding units will know where to go, and the RTO can broadcast our location to anyone who wasn't already enroute.

We both exit the car and approach the guy. I quickly pat him down to verify he has no weapons in his pants and then I handcuff him while Gina begins asking him questions, mainly name and birthday. She sits back in the car and runs him for wants and warrants and to verify his identity on our MDC (mobile digital computer). I remain outside the car and make idle conversation with him while she handles the computer.

"You know you never would have gotten jammed up if you hadn't been messing with your dick out in public, you know that, right?"

"Yeah I know, I messed up. You're not gonna tell my PO (parole officer), are you?"

"We'll see what my partner finds."

"My PO is gonna be mad if he finds out I got in trouble."

"Did you kill anybody or anything recently?"

"What?! No way!"

"Then I'm ok with giving you a warning, but we'll see what she finds."

"Did that guy want you to arrest me?"

I reply, "Nobody wants to make a citizen's arrest, they just want you to stop, so you had better promise you'll stop and not make us come back out here again. I don't want to get any calls later about some guy jacking off in front of a corner store."

He nods with a grin, laughing sheepishly. Good reaction, that's the kind of rapport I was going for. Better to have them smiling and at ease than tense and ready to fight me. "What are you on parole for?"

He tilts his head slightly as if trying to find the words. "It was like a sex thing."

"Oh. Got it. So you obviously didn't learn your lesson."

"I mean, I wasn't, I didn't mean to –

"You don't have to explain it to me, you just gotta stay out of trouble."

He smiles and nods again and looks off. "I like your partner. She has nice eyes. She's pretty."

"Yeah, most people like her."

"You think she'd give me her number?"

"She's already married."

"No way! I'd still take her out."

I shake my head, "I don't think you're her type."

"What you talking about man, of course I'm her type!"

"You weren't wearing pants just two minutes ago."

The interaction is going smoothly enough. I don't want an arrest – we have bigger plans for the night. Also, food. Besides, this guy obviously isn't all there, I can tell by the way he speaks, avoids eye contact, his general demeanor. Not to mention he was just rubbing one out not even five minutes ago. Gina steps back out the car.

"He's got warrants."

He protests, "What? No way, I just checked in today!"

She replies, "You must have missed your appointment or something, because this warrant was *issued* today, and it is specifically for missing your check-in."

"Damn, we gotta take you bro. Tell you what, we'll just take you for the warrant, no open charge, fair?"

"You're not gonna tell my PO about this, right? He'll be mad."

"No, we're not gonna tell him about the jacking off thing, just don't do it anymore. He'll contact you from the jail, you'll be out in a day or two, just taking you on the warrant."

Gina tells me, "He's a 290." 290 PC is the code that requires someone to register as a sex offender. I reply, "Yeah he just said he was on parole for some sex thing, didn't get into details."

Tonight we're driving a cage-less black and white Ford Crown Victoria. It's the best car you can check out from the kitroom, mainly because there's space to stretch out. In the normal patrol Crown Vics or the Explorer SUVs, there is a windowed partition which separates the officers in the front seat from the suspects who ride in the back. The back seat is a hard plastic, easy to clean up and sanitize as opposed to having a cushion. Most people who get arrested tend to be under the influence, sweaty, generally smelly and in desperate need of a shower, or oozing one or another of bodily fluids, and nobody wants that getting stuck in a backseat cushion. The partition also means that the officers in the front have a natural barrier of protection from someone who is less than cooperative in the back.

The only bad thing about a partitioned car is you can't really stretch out or recline your seat comfortably. As a specialized unit, we had the option of checking out one of the cage-less cars, because in a specialized unit it's not uncommon to ride "three deep," usually when the unit has an odd man out. In a specialized unit where your main job is pro-active enforcement, where it is more likely you will be confronting a group of suspects or gang members, it's always nice to have an extra set of eyes, handcuffs, and gun in the car. An officer riding solo isn't going to be expected to put in work the way they would if they had a partner or two, simply for safety's sake.

We lucked out and checked out a cage-less car, perfect for comfort in that we were going to be doing some more covert-level surveillance and could use the flexibility of having more space. The only downside was if we got a body, the passenger officer would have to sit in the backseat with the arrestee during the transport. Again, since there was no partition, it was a measure of safety for the driver – if the arrestee acted up, there was at least somebody back there with them to control the situation and have the driver's back.

Gina sits our guy down on the passenger side in the back seat and begins asking him questions, filling out the rest of his FI (field identification) card. I grab his backpack and begin searching through it for any contraband on the hood of the car. Again, all fairly routine. We're both a bit annoyed. So much for our plans for the night, right out the gate and already a body. And a gross one at that, a perv. We can get food after, hopefully this doesn't take long. At least it's a felony.

While searching through the backpack, I hear some arguing. I look up and see Gina, standing by the car, and she appears to be going back and forth with our guy, arguing about God knows what. I can see she's annoyed. "I'm a police officer. I'm a woman, that is so disrespectful."

I shake my head and ignore it, continuing my search. I finish the search and toss the backpack in the trunk and climb into the driver seat. Gina closes the door and sits in the back seat next to our guy. I take one look in the rearview mirror and I can read her face. Up until now, we'd been working together for quite a while and I knew not much rattled her. As a female street cop especially, you tend to develop a thick skin because you take so much more abuse than your male counterparts. Not to mention, Gina was way prettier than most female coppers. Petite with an athletic frame from years of playing competitive soccer and with a distinctly feminine voice, she had green eyes. We used to joke that her eyes sparkled. We would even joke with arrestees when they were trying to describe that one female officer with the eyes who arrested them, we would help them out —

"The one with the green eyes?"

"Yeah, the one with the green eyes, they were sparkly, that's her!"

"Yeah, we know who she is, I'll track her down."

I take one look at her and I sense a level of discomfort I had never before seen in her. She looks visibly shaken but trying to maintain a cool demeanor. I ask her, "You wanna switch for the transport?"

She nods yes without missing a beat. "Just put on your gloves and don't let him touch anything."

I put on some latex gloves and we switch spots. She puts the car in gear and we start on our way back to the station.

Now remember, we are only a block away from the station. We need to go around a couple of blocks to get back because of the one-way streets. As I'm sitting next to the guy I can tell he's getting more and more uncomfortable, maybe he has a bit of claustrophobia setting in.

"Hey, just keep it together man, we're right around the corner from the station, easy process here."

"Yeah ok, I just don't like being in cars for long."

"No worries, we'll be there in no time."

Gina makes eye contact with me through the rear view. I motion to her with my head and eyes, saying without speaking the words, move it partner, eat a few lights. Last thing either of us wants is for this guy to freak out in the back seat of the car.

We make it back to the station without incident. She pulls into the garage, past the officer sitting in the guard shack on his phone, and into the booking stalls. I help the guy out of the car, she grabs his backpack from the trunk, and we start walking him inside. We're both doing mental math, making a time estimate of how long this whole process is going to take. We're both hungry and getting more and more annoyed we stumbled into this one. I'm thinking thirty minutes tops to get the booking approval and his rap sheet printed out here at the station. I can do that while she handles his property. Five to ten minute trip to MDC (Metropolitan Detention Center, the actual jail where arrestees are booked). Hopefully it's quick there, twenty minutes if we're lucky and he has no medical issues, then we can book him drop-n-go and be out of there in maybe thirty minutes. What's that, less than ninety minutes all in? Ok, there's still a good bit of the night left, maybe forty-five minutes to eat after that, then back to our original plan.

We walk up to the window by the watch commander's office. Gina begins filling out his info on the log-in sheet while the watch commander comes out and asks, "What do you guys got?"

"Felony warrants."

"Felony warrants, good stuff," says the sergeant. He asks our guy, "Sir, do you know why you're here?"

"Yes."

"Are you sick, ill or injured?"

"No, but I do need to see a doctor at the jail, I have a condition."

"Ok these officers will make sure that happens. Any other questions for me?"

"No sir."

"Alright, cooperate with these officers and they'll get you processed, best of luck to you."

Shit, he needs medical. Hopefully there's not a big line. That's always the wild card, could be a quick ten minute thing or a four hour fiasco if he's got something more serious. This could turn into an end of watch caper. Crossing our fingers...

Into the report writing room. Central Station's report writing room, oddly enough, is rarely used to actually write reports. It's more of a processing room. It isn't huge, maybe thirty feet by thirty feet, about the size of an average office space. On one wall there are cubbies full of admin paperwork – various report templates, booking sheets, medical questionnaires, bail computation forms. Perpendicular to the cubbies are three rows of desks, each with about three computer workstations per row, with enough space in between each to lay out and inventory evidence, personal property, or miscellaneous paperwork.

At the end of the rows of desks is a long bench spanning the length of the wall, with metal loops so arrestees can be handcuffed to the bench. In all, there is maybe space for around seven or eight arrestees. Behind everything, there are two holding tanks, each with a large plexiglass panel so you can see in and out. Inside each tank there is a metal bench again with handcuff loops. It's all for the purpose of flexibility and convenience. Sometimes it's necessary to separate arrestees from each other. We may not want them talking to each other, or it may just be to appease a simple request of someone feeling more comfortable, that they would rather sit alone for a few minutes. Not to mention, in the tank we can safely take the handcuffs off, though it's not a requirement. Little things like these are all tools to make everyone's lives easier.

Crazy thing is that because there is so much traffic coming through, the room is always chaotic, with all the wide variety of Skid Row personalities being processed for pre-booking. Imagine seven arrestees sitting on the bench. Two are gangsters, arrested on a gun charge. Two are dope dealers. Two are crackheads who got caught up in the game and were somehow roped into the sales case with the dealers. One is detained on a 5150 hold for trying to run into traffic. Of the seven, two have used crack cocaine within the last four hours, and two are coming off their highs from meth which they each smoked two days ago. Doesn't matter which ones. Oh, and I forgot to mention the one "normal" guy who got arrested at Macy's for shoplifting. He's not homeless and not a career criminal – he's just stupid and got caught. That's eight. And they're all talking shit to each other. It's damn near impossible to write a coherent report in this room with so many distractions, so most officers go back to the detective offices to write their reports.

I walk our guy into the report writing room to sit him on the bench. He asks, "Can you sit me in the tank? I don't like being around other people."

I have no reason to deny him, fine with me as long as they're not occupied. I walk him to the back, past about three other arrestees sitting on the bench, their arresting officers in various stages of the admin process. I sit him in the tank, still handcuffed behind his back.

"Aww come on, you can't take the cuffs off?"

"No, not this time man, I know what you're gonna start doing."

He'd turn that tank into a semen covered hazmat scene.

I lock him in the tank and head over to one of the workstations. Gina is already going through his property and packaging it to book with him. She still looks disgusted. I log into the system and run his name, pull the warrants, print out his rap sheet, start filling out the booking paperwork. I take a glance back to check on our guy. While seated at the computer, I can see him through the plexiglass from his stomach up. He's got no shirt on, and I can see him wiggling around. Something's off.

I stand up and walk back there, and what do I find but this guy sitting there with his pants at his ankles. I'm in shock. I start yelling at him from outside the tank.

"Why are your pants off! Why would you do that?!"

As if he had an answer.

He starts stammering, trying to offer an explanation that wouldn't make sense even he was speaking clearly.

"Pull them back up, now!"

"Ok, ok, I'll pull them up, I'll pull them up."

He starts trying to wiggle his legs and shimmy the pants which are wrapped around his ankles back up to his waist. But he's still handcuffed and they won't go up. He's stuck.

"I can't get them up."

"Well you got them off, pull them up!"

He struggles some more before giving up.

"I need help."

"Goddammit!" I open the door and put on another pair of gloves. I help him wrestle the pants back up his legs.

"Now don't do that again! Every time you do something like that back here it makes this all take longer! I could have been finishing your packet to get you out of here!"

"Ok, ok, I'm sorry, I won't do it again."

Gina is shaking her head. The other officers in the room are laughing hysterically. The arrestees start chiming in, "You fools brought a crazy motherfucker up in here, didn't you! All nasty!"

I start back into the paperwork, ever more annoyed. We could have been eating dinner by now.

When a couple minutes later, I hear a voice call out from another officer, "Your guy is doing a thing again."

I turn around and look back at the tank. Again, from my chair I can see our guy, shirtless, with only his stomach up to his head visible, now bouncing up and down in a disturbingly repetitive motion. The expression on his face is one of focus. I know I'm about to ask a dangerous question, an answer to which I know will only upset me.

I call out to him, "What are you doing?"

"I've got my thumb in my ass!"

"Well pull it out!"

"Ok!"

Here's where it all takes a surreal turn. I'm sure nobody could have heard it in actuality, but I swear I could have heard an audible *plop*. The sound made from the suction of a thumb being rapidly removed from a butthole.

"Sonofabitch! This fucking guy!"

Gina looks over, "That's what he was doing in the car when I was trying to interview him. Fucking gross!"

The report writing room is a riot right now, arrestees on the bench doubled over in laughter, their arresting officers laughing just as hard, looking at us with zero envy, just glad they aren't the ones who brought in a guy with an uncontrollable impulse to finger his own asshole while handcuffed.

We somehow manage to regain focus and finish up his paperwork. Gina signs him out. I glove up yet again and make my way back to the tank. Thankfully, there are no fingers in any holes and his pants are pulled up the whole way. I grab him and walk him out the room to the jeers of the arrestees, "Make that nigga wash his hands, with his nasty feces ass fingers!" They weren't wrong.

Back into the car to transport him to the jail. I'm in the back again, Gina gets in the driver seat. "Just fucking get us to the jail, drive fast."

She exits the garage and steps on the gas with a bit more urgency. I just don't want mister doodoo fingers here to freak out on me, remembering he doesn't like cars. The less time we spend in the car the better. We're only in the car for maybe thirty seconds when he starts bouncing rhythmically again. Oh no. His pants are still up and I can see his hands, so nothing is inserted anywhere. Yet. Dear God just let us get to the jail.

When out of nowhere he starts singing.

"Sometimes I feel I've got to…run away, I've got to…get away from the pain you drive into the heart of me, the love we share, seems to go nowhere, and I've lost my light, for I toss and turn I can't sleep at night."

Is this really happening? I see Gina's eyes in the rear view. Mutual confusion.

"Once I ran to you, now I run from you, this tainted love you've given, I gave you all a boy could give, take my tears and that's not really all! Tainted love, whooaa!"

Without missing a lyric. Every single fucking lyric to "Tainted Love." By Soft Cell. And the rhythm of the bouncing, perfectly to the song, matching up with the rhythm from the tank. Is that what he was thinking? Was that what he was hearing in his head as he thumbed his own anus? I've had songs stuck in my head before, I mean we all have, but Jesus Christ…

We pull into the garage at MDC. He's made it through the whole verse.

Gina says to him, "You're not a bad singer."

"Thank you!"

I make eye contact with her through the mirror with a look that says "Are you serious? This can't be real," and from those sparkly eyes I can tell there's a smile on her face, stifling laughter. But now I'm the one with the disgusted uncomfortable look, and she can definitely tell. How the tables have turned.

As we're walking into the jail, past the petty thieves and domestic abusers and crackheads and drunks, all in their various phases of processing, we make our way back to medical. Lucky for us, there is one person currently being seen by the nursing staff and one other person in the queue in front of us.

"Sit down next to her," I say.

He sits down next to a woman likely in her mid-thirties, except she looks like she's in her mid-fifties. The streets will add anywhere from fifteen to twenty years onto your appearance. The transformation is stunning, to see someone new to the area, young and healthy, well kempt, completely transform within only a few weeks' time. That's how you become institutionalized – the streets get to you, and you just get stuck. She's there on a misdemeanor warrant for something like shoplifting or simple possession.

The woman has ratty dark brown hair adorned with a hodgepodge of old ribbons, and wearing a torn jean skirt over mismatched stockings. She's not in a complete state of homelessness – probably been bouncing back and forth between hotels, tents, and friends' apartments for at least the last six months. She has most of her teeth but not all of them, and her skin is worn and colorless. That's all from the meth. It's all adding up, because her eyes tell that same story. They're batting left and right, paranoid, anxious. She is twitching her leg up and down rapidly, a nervous tick. She's probably still tweaking, and that's why she's headed to medical.

Our guy is sitting next to her on a plastic waiting room chair. He's not in the car, but her anxiousness seems to be wearing on him, like it's almost contagious. He's looking like he did in the car, shifting in his seat, like the walls are closing in slowly. We recognize it. Gotta get him talking, gotta distract him so this all goes smoothly. We still need to eat.

Gina goes first, "What was that song you were singing earlier in the car? Who sings that?"

I reply, "I'm not sure who sings it, but it's one of those eighties classics, always on the radio."

Our guy switches gears and leaps back into the conversation, "Yeah it's the band Soft Cell, it's a really good song."

The crazy lady jumps into the conversation. "Which song?"

"You should sing it for her." Gina gestures with her head towards our guy, suggesting he should start singing.

He jumps right back into the second verse from where he left off in the car, bobbing his head and rocking his body in the seat. "Now I know I've got to…run away, I've got to…get away, you don't really want anymore from me, to make things right, you need someone to hold you tight, and you think love is to pray, but I'm sorry I don't pray that way!"

Our girl is bobbing along, that anxious empty smile turning into something recognizable from a pre-Skid Row past. They're perfectly matched, in all the strangeness. It's like how comedian Jim Gaffigan would describe, "Like two dirty pairs of underwear."

"Tainted love!" the lady exclaims. I guess she knows the song. "Don't touch me please, I cannot stand the way you teeaase!"

"See, she knows it!" Gina gestures towards our girl. Her arresting officers have been standing next to us this whole time, giving off an air of general disinterest. They definitely got stuck with this caper against their better wishes.

"That part doesn't come yet, the chorus happens first! Tainted love, whooaa!"

"I know the fucking lyrics! I know the song. She just said I know the song." She gestures towards Gina, almost as if it's her job to confirm whether or not she is qualified to know or sing the lyrics.

"If you knew it you would get it right, I was the one singing it," replies our guy.

She comes back, "I'm allowed to fucking sing too!"

"Then get it right, you bitch!"

This is not happening, how are they arguing? Why is the nurse taking so long? Call her in already…

I tell our guy, "Why don't you sit in this seat over here, give her a little space, she seems upset over the song. He shifts over to the adjacent seat, taking my suggestion. A few moments of silence. More silence. What place is going to be open by the time we finish here? Maybe we can grab a slice from Joe's…

Then they both start shifting in their seats again. That anxiety starts creeping its way back into the corridor. They're already both fucking crazy, last thing we all need is for them to start fighting each other. Where is the nurse? What's the next move? Diffuse it before they freak out, I gotta do something or we're never going to eat…

"Ba dum bum bum…bum bum…sometimes I feel, I've got to…bum bum…run away, I've got to…bum bum…get away —

I start into the song. Our guy joins in and takes over. And then our girl joins in. We're a goddamn musical trio singing eighties hits in a jail. Thumb in his ass guy, meth head chick, and me, the uniformed police officer. They sing in unison like fucking Johnny and June Cash, and there I am singing the staccato synthesizer part, keeping time for these two maniacs. The other officers are no longer disinterested. They're smiling and letting out a few chuckles. One of them says to us, "You guys *gotta* be from Central, maybe Hollywood." I nod, "You called it, Central." Gina is beside herself. She turns away from the arrestees and looks directly at me, hands over her mouth to keep her laughs from becoming audible.

"Tainted love…"

And then my lyric, "Whooaa!"

Like two dirty pairs of underwear. And I'm the guy doing the laundry.

We make it through medical without any further actual incident and eventually book our guy. Not to say it still wasn't all surreal, coming off of our vocal rendition of Soft Cell's "Tainted Love" and walking back to the nurse's station. The attending nurse, "Were you guys the ones singing?"

"Yeah, that was us."

"You guys weren't half bad."

"Right."

We couldn't escape the fact that our guy had his thumb up his ass less than an hour ago, and was jerking himself off pantless in the middle of the street not much long before that. He was gross and creepy. Shirtless, chubby, unshaven, stinky, and still horny. Every woman who passed us in the jail, be it a nurse, an arrestee, a detention officer, he would lick his lips and blow kisses. Like I said before, it takes a lot to get under the skin of a street cop or a woman who works the jails, but each woman was utterly disgusted, not even wanting to be in the vicinity of this guy. Something about his look was just violating.

Most women can be disgusted by a guy in the moment, but what really gets under the skin is knowing he's going to be pleasuring himself to the thought of them later. And not in the way of an empty threat just to purposefully disrespect someone – it was unnerving because he *didn't* say it, they *knew* that's what he was thinking, and they *knew* he was dead serious. That's what Gina felt in the car, and I could tell just from a look. You might not know each other's names, but spend enough time with someone and you start speaking the same language. Oddly enough, the only one he hadn't hit on was his duet partner. I guess that wouldn't have been kosher, like it was too taboo even for him.

*   *   *

Look up the music video to "Tainted Love" and you'll find two official music videos, something I didn't know was a thing until I discovered it myself. One is completely trippy, much what you would expect from an early eighties production. Wild colors, cheap looking special digital effects. It looks like a synthesizer got high and hallucinated the video itself. The other video is even more bizarre and is actually a little more fitting to the lyrics. The video is set in either ancient or early-20th century times, the main singer is a guy wearing a toga, and a woman, presumably his wife, is dressed like Jane Austen. They're sitting outside of what looks like a Greek or Roman villa, and for some reason they're at an outdoor table having afternoon tea. It all has a very British cosplaying as Greek vibe. There's a buff, shirtless black guy who's presumably a slave holding a fan shade over the white couple. The guy starts singing, and we are introduced to a little girl of about eight years old, who is notably a mixed-race child and for some reason is also wearing a toga. She isn't nearly as dark as the slave, but has curly brown hair and a mulatto skin tone. The implication is that the mother had an affair with the black guy, and now the main white guy who's singing is addressing the mother, noting their "tainted love," the personification in the little girl. Call it a relic of the time. Back in the eighties, mixed race couples were still considered taboo and not wholly accepted, not to mention the no man's land of racial ambiguity where the children would come to inhabit. How fitting, our own surreal moment existing in a state of ambiguity where all you can do is nod along and keep pressing forward.

And that's where the song sits with me years later. Not just the casual meaning of the song, but it really *means* what it's trying to say, at least to me. Social taboo, sexual deviance, perversion. I dare you to try having a professional conversation with a man who is repeatedly pleasuring his own asshole. Sitting there, literally with his thumb up his ass. Do it on an empty stomach. Now imagine yourself singing a catchy pop song with this same person. Then take a step back and re-evaluate your life decisions that have brought you to this point, because this is now your reality. Surreal enough?

I don't remember how the rest of that shift played out. We finished booking, regained our composure, asked each other if that was real or if we were in some kind of extradimensional Twilight Zone episode. We laughed it away. It's just another Central caper, another day in Skid Row. We'll come back tomorrow and it'll still be there, with all the same oddball characters, the same smells, the same images, the same hot spots, and all with mostly just slight degrees of variation.

I want to say we got a bite to eat, hit up some of our other partners and met up for a cup of coffee during a second field roll call, but I can't say for sure who was there or where we went. I want to say we told them the story, that they reacted with both disbelief *and* a lack of surprise, believing without a shadow of a doubt that this all actually happened. They likely told us what they had gotten into, and more likely than not, the original plans we all had for the night had probably shifted so much by then that we all would have had to wait until the next night anyway. And after loading back into our cars, and after countless other shifts since then, only some of the details stick with you, while others fade.

Yet somehow, whenever I turn on a radio and a certain song starts to play, it all comes back – the smells, the images, the disgust, the taste of the coffee afterwards. I can recall it all so vividly. And even amidst all of that, no matter how hard I try to remember, no matter how much I rack my brain, the one thing I can't remember is the guy's name. Fucking Soft Cell.

The Shrug

I always tell people there are generally at least four versions of every story. There's one side's version, the other side's version, what actually happened, and the version that goes in the police report.

If you walk into the records department of almost any police station, you'll notice one thing: there are a shit ton of papers. Generally speaking, you're going to find hard copies of every report that's been written in the last couple years at a minimum, and when you think of a large American city like Los Angeles, you can imagine how high the stack can get. On an average shift, an LAPD patrol unit will rack up maybe three to four reports, ranging from simple vandalism to rape, robbery, shots fired, and everything in between. Multiply that out by an average of maybe five units per shift, then multiply that out by four overlapping patrol shifts per day, and so on and so forth. Do this and you can see how much paper is actually flowing.

You'd come out to about seventy odd reports per day per division, and that's just from patrol. Granted, some divisions are bigger than others, with really large main day and night watch deployments and smaller swing shifts, others are more evenly distributed. Some divisions are incredibly fast paced and busy, others are slow. It all just depends on the particular area.

To further complicate things, this doesn't include specialized units like vice, narcotics, gangs, or detectives, who all may be working on follow-ups to patrol investigations or unrelated cases not tied to radio calls for service. They may not even be tied to one particular division, as some of these units work city wide. It doesn't include the internal paperwork of officer involved shootings or traffic collisions, internal affairs complaints, or strategic findings from the brass. But the one thing that does unify all of these reports is that at their core, each of them tells a story.

With that level of volume, it all has to serve some purpose, right? Nobody is taking reports for the sake of taking reports, even though to the average cop it often feels that way. Each report is telling a particular story to a very specific audience. You see, because police work isn't about gunfights, high speed chases, undercover stings, or for that matter, simply serving the public. Sure, all of these things do happen, some more often than others, but what it's really all about is conveying events and stating what happened – ergo, policework is all about storytelling.

To account for the sheer volume of reports being written and stories being told, there needs to be some streamlining factors so a human whose job it is to review them can actually make some sense of it all. Further complicate it by throwing in legal jargon and official policy directives that everything needs to adhere to and it adds another layer of depth. The writing itself, the tools of the storytelling, takes on a certain pattern and a hyper-specific type of language develops – that's what most people come to know as "cop speak." Officers become engaged in a pursuit. An officer involved shooting occurs. Someone observes a suspect remove the item and conceal it within his backpack and exit the store past open cash registers without attempting to pay. The language defines the action and establishes the relevant elements. It's factual, impersonal, no frills.

Next, we see structure and consistency become the driving factors in the storytelling. Each report reads like a thousand before it. First section, Source of Activity. On November 3, 2017 my partner, officer Gina #12345 and I, officer Santiago #12346, were assigned to uniformed patrol, working Central Division, watch five. We received a radio call of a robbery just occurred at the corner of Same Shit and Different Day. Next is the Investigation section. Upon arrival, we made contact with the victim, who stated the exact elements of the crime that occurred using the exact legal verbiage that the filing team cares about which will ensure a conviction to a really picky district attorney.

Nobody ever says, "The suspect approached me, brandished a black handgun and demanded money. In fear for my life, I handed the suspect my wallet, at which point he fled the scene and I immediately called the police." Usually it just comes out as, "I was walking minding my own business, and this nigga think he gon' come out and rob me?! Fuck that! What you gon' do about that? Why you ain't catch him? You fucking cops out here fucking with people over some bullshit, people out here robbing motherfuckers with guns!"

"What did he look like?"

"Look at the cameras, goddamn!"

Then come the other relevant subheadings, usually Medical Treatment, Court Availability, Additional Information, and maybe Arrest, Booking, Use of Force, or Evidence, if any of it is applicable. Most crime reports follow the same structure for the simple sake of ensuring that the relevant information makes it to the detective's desk and can be interpreted quickly. Nobody needs all the details. Like I said before, it's true, but it's only a certain version of the truth. That's that fourth version, the one that makes it into the police report. Shorthand shortcuts, if you will.

The formatting and style come to dictate how most cops see the world. Most people who are immersed in this language and method of storytelling begin experiencing the world through this lens of language and formatting. It isn't just cops, it's anyone who does anything for long enough. In a lot of ways, you become what you do unless you make an active effort to ground yourself outside of your work. And through this, you lose a lot of the real truth of a story. You don't glean any of its essence that makes it real – you don't really *get* it.

This is how it usually plays out. Something shitty happens, say a couple of masked gunmen storm into a liquor store to stick up the register and make off with a bag full of cash, maybe they fired a warning shot through the ceiling and unbeknownst to them, shot and killed someone in an apartment upstairs. The first call goes out from the store owner.

"911, what's your emergency?"

The store owner relays what happened, he says a couple guys came in, shot up his store and stole all the money from the register. He doesn't think anyone is hurt, but he needs the police. He describes the men, what they were wearing, what he could tell of their race. He mentions what he can recall of the car they sped off in, and even a partial plate. He says the one guy fired off a shotgun and the other guy had a black handgun, but he didn't shoot.

That's the first story.

Meanwhile, a second call is made from the upstairs neighbor. Old man was just sitting in his living room watching tv when he heard some yelling downstairs in the store, next thing he knows a giant hole rips through the floor and strikes his wife, and she's bleeding and just hurry and send an ambulance.

That's the second story.

Three more similar calls of shots fired come out, with multiple reports of a vehicle leaving at a high rate of speed. All the descriptions are piecemeal, two calls had matching descriptions of the car but no plate, one call only heard the shots and saw three guys running out the store, but didn't see if anyone jumped in a car. He did see a car speeding away, but it was a different color than the one the other guys said.

We'll call this all the third story.

Three very similar stories, all fairly consistent in that they depict a shooting, but none of them are perfect. All mostly true, but most definitely not the whole picture.

All of these stories get relayed from the dispatcher on the line with the caller to the RTO, who broadcasts the calls to patrol units in the area of shots fired, robbery suspects just left, possible victim down. They broadcast the description of the suspects and cars, but even that information is only partial. By the time patrol officers arrive on scene and clear it for the ambulance to come in and assist the victim, the suspects are long gone. The coppers start asking around and gathering statements. Turns out the old lady upstairs didn't make it, so now it's a homicide and it's time to secure the crime scene. Up with the yellow tape, and our guys make requests for additional units and a supervisor.

Supervisor arrives on scene and starts managing. He makes a call to notify the watch commander they just had a homicide. Watch commander calls the captain who is at home to notify him. If you're keeping track, that's the fourth and fifth time a version of the story has been told, and the first report hasn't even been written yet. But each time the story is relayed, it changes ever so slightly up until that first report gets written. The homicide detectives eventually arrive on scene to take over the investigation while everyone else defaults into a supporting role, whether it be blocking traffic, keeping the crowd back, taking statements. Eventually one of those detectives writes an official report and it gets put into a special binder, what detectives call a murder book, which has all the paperwork and documents relevant to a particular case. This is the first time the actual story is officially documented, yet it is the sixth time the story has been told.

Here's where it gets interesting. After piecing it all together and exhausting the leads that night, detectives get to work detecting. Assuming the best-case scenario, after a few days they're able to pull off some crackerjack police work and find some informants, comb through some databases, fill in the gaps, and eventually manage to identify the perpetrators. They get to work on writing a warrant affidavit. The affidavit is basically a beginning to end summary of how it all played out, from the time the initial calls came out to when those first patrol cops showed up to when detectives took over the scene, did the follow ups, and ultimately solved the case. They lay it out for a judge, and when the judge reads it, that judge is going to believe there is enough evidence to establish probable cause that the identified suspects are in fact the perpetrators of the crime. Judge signs the warrant, it gets entered into the statewide warrant system, and eventually somebody brings them in.

Nice job, case closed, right? Not so fast. That warrant was just another version of the story, a version to get the case to a court, where it will ultimately go before a jury, at which point more and more versions of the story are going to be told. You see, the affidavit was a story told specifically to the judge, so it included all the parts the judge was interested in, namely establishing identity and what we call the fruits of the crime, all needing to adhere to established legal standards. Because they aren't trying to get an arrest warrant simply for a killing or a murder, they are trying to get an arrest warrant for violating Section 187 of the California Penal Code, which has very specific elements that need to be satisfied.

But the jury is a different beast. They are going to hear a version that never made it into the affidavit. They are going to hear stories about how the old man and the old lady were stalwart members of the community, advocated for civil rights, were active members in the church, fostered three kids and served dinners to the homeless with their grandchildren every Thanksgiving, and how these criminals who so brazenly robbed the store, not only robbed an honest local business, but robbed the community of one of its most revered members.

Another part that got left out was the fact that one of the defendants had just turned eighteen and didn't even have a gun. He was just waiting for his older cousin and his friend to come back out the store and didn't know they were going to do anything. He had his whole life ahead of him, was on track to attend junior college, and is really just as much a victim as the old lady. Sad because at least she had lived most of her life, so really if this kid goes to jail on a murder rap, it's like two lives have been lost. What's on trial here is a system that tries victims and doesn't deliver justice, because he wasn't really the one who did it.

Then another version of the story is told by the arresting officers – not the officers who responded first to the scene, but the officers who happened to run the car's license plate days later and attempted to pull it over because it matched the description from the shooting. The driver took them on a high-speed pursuit because he panicked, not knowing they were even wanted for murder. Maybe this was a key piece that detectives used to identify the rest of the suspects, ultimately placing them all in the car and at scene the night of the shooting, and leading to that warrant.

In court, the arresting officer tells exactly what happened, but not in English. It's in cop speak. He's very matter of fact. While conducting extra patrol near the intersection of Wherever and Where's That, officers observed a vehicle matching the description of a vehicle wanted in connection to a shooting that took place days earlier. When officers attempted to pull over the vehicle to conduct an investigative stop, the driver failed to yield and accelerated through the intersection in an attempt to evade the officers. The officers engaged in a pursuit through the neighboring areas for approximately five minutes, at which point officers conducted a pursuit intervention technique which was effective in bringing the pursuit to an end. The suspect was detained without further incident. The driver arrested is identified before this court as defendant sitting at the end table with counsel.

All of these stories are entirely true, all telling parts but never the whole version of the same story. But you can see how from beginning to end, the story changes for the intended audience. And you can see how police work is all about storytelling. That's the end game.

There's one part that never actually gets documented in the official record, but make no mistake, it most definitely finds an audience. This audience hears this version at 3am in a 7-11 parking lot, and it is arguably one of the truest versions there is.

It starts as a casual conversation amongst six tired officers working on a quiet night. They decide to meet up for a cup because they're all fighting the sandman. The entire division is asleep, it's dead out. Nobody to pull over, no calls to respond to, just plain dead. It doesn't get any more dead than it is now. What these guys wouldn't give for something to happen. Somebody commit a crime already.

Two cars pull into the lot first. They all walk inside, greet the cashier, make some idle chit chat about how it's finally nice to have a quiet moment, but deep down everyone is jonesing for something to happen, or for the night to just hurry up and end already. They grab their hot drinks and head outside. The coffees are all black, the bitter taste matches the mood. Except for Pete, he loads his coffee up with sugar and whipped cream and chocolate syrup, looks more like a dessert than a cup of coffee. There's always *that* guy.

They step outside and cluster around the still warm engine of their black and white.

"You guys get anything tonight?"

"Couple reports, nothing crazy. A vandalism and a burg, you know that antique shop on Pacific?"

"Yeah, across from the school."

"Some guys broke into it, stole the register, broke some glass. I think they took off once the alarm went off, didn't want to stick around too long."

A third car pulls into the lot and two other coppers emerge. They nod at the other four clustered around the black and white and head into the store to grab their coffees.

"Hey, you guys remember the pursuit of that 187 suspect a while back? The guy who shot that old lady from the downstairs market?"

"Yeah, what about it?"

"We're in a whole world of shit over it."

The other officers make their way back out the store with their hot drinks, desperate to inject some liveliness into their evening. Only three hours til end of watch, people will start waking up in around two...

"So primary puts out the backup, they're following this guy and he takes off, we start hauling ass towards the pursuit. They're driving on west 7th, but we hear west Lemon, so my partner here is blowing through lights and stop signs, code three, full on lights and sirens, the works. And we're getting farther and farther away from it. And their broadcast isn't that great, so we're just trying to get our bearings, and eventually it's like what the fuck, where is everybody? There should at least be some other cars. So we give up, shut it all down."

"That sucks."

"Turns out, when they go to pull everybody's in car video for the pursuit review, they pull ours since we were going code three the whole time, and what do they find? They see us blasting through red lights and stop signs! And when the audio kicks in, all they hear is this guy swearing like he's back in the Navy, fucking idiots, putting out the wrong fucking address, it's all fucked up this and that, dumb shits don't know where they are, you get it. Makes us look like a bunch of assholes. Anyway, we got subpoenaed for the case because we were listed in the pursuit. We talk to the DA, we don't actually know anything, we never made it to the scene, so he's asking why we're even there and we say we were hoping he could tell us, so he kicks us loose."

"You guys at least catch any overtime on it?"

"Yeah, we got some overtime. Then go figure, I'm turning in my slip the next day and the sergeant flags me down, says we're both catching beefs for the pursuit, said we were driving in an *unsafe manner* and using profanity. Of course, we weren't actually in the pursuit, but we still got hemmed up anyway."

"Why they even making a big deal of it?"

"It's a murder case, so defense is gonna subpoena every video and they don't want to get embarrassed so they gotta jam us on it. I explain the DA just kicked us loose that very day. Doesn't matter, paperwork's coming down."

"Never fails, that's how they get you. Makes zero difference, but they gotta fuck somebody."

This is the part that never gets documented. This is the perspective everybody misses, the confused direction it all spins, roping in all the unsuspecting entities and creating a whole new version of reality. But what's the part that makes this the truest version of them all? It doesn't actually come with these guys sharing the story, it happens just after. At the *very* end. They shake their heads, shrug, and another guy starts into another story. An alarm call comes out across town, they pound back the rest of their coffees, get back into their cars and head to the call to keep the night moving along. And they never revisit the issue again. Never mind that somebody died, that's ancillary to the truth here. The real truth is that it's not worth getting tore up about, because in reality it's just another in a long series. There will be plenty more pursuits and arrests and court cases, that's the whole point, and somehow each one will spin in some wildly unpredictable direction. And realistically, you can't do anything about it. The lady got killed. These guys went the wrong way and managed to get a complaint out of it. The driver who got arrested is gonna take a deal anyway and name the shooter. Then it's a shrug and onto the next one.

I always look for the shrug when someone gets to the end of a story and I try to place it, because I find that's usually where I identify the main point. It usually happens at the end, or at least *by* the end, but not always. If by the end of it, the person telling the story really got at the truth, there's not much else to do other than shrug and move on. Because that's reality – the world keeps spinning, it doesn't slow down for our sensibilities, it doesn't stop to ponder the right and wrong or the emotion of it, it's already happened and we're just left with its memory, the experience of feeling it, the several different versions making up the collage that comes together to form its true essence. There's just nothing left to say because it's already been said. Coffee's getting cold, get on with things.

That's not to say each different version can't contain some element of that truth. Sure, it's absolutely tragic that the lady died, and it's tragic that the kid didn't know what was going to happen. Hopefully justice ends up being served. But that's not the *point*. The point is that it's all a product of the same system, the intertwining happenstances. *Everyone* has gotten roped in, whether they wanted to or not...even you, because remember, this story isn't even real. A true story that never happened, which is somehow more true than all the documented versions of reality. Everyone gets roped in, and *that's* the real shrug.

First Impressions, Lasting Impressions

I've always been intrigued by the idea of the first impression. The first handshake, the first introduction to your soon to be in-laws. You've got one shot, like the Eminem song – mom's spaghetti something or other, he's nervous, you've heard it. It's that moment when you walk into the house party and survey the scene – is it going to be worth hanging around, or should you start looking for an out? You start piecing it together asking and answering questions, filling in the blanks as you go – this party's dead, why is there so much flannel, where are all the good-looking people? Why is there no food? Where are the drinks? What's the deal with the music? Why is that guy drinking milk right out the jug? What is happening? It all tells a story.

It's that moment when you go up to the bar to break the ice with the one girl who's been eyeing you for the better part of a half hour, and the first thing out of your mouth is your name, except you goof it up and mispronounce it, and now you're desperately backtracking and trying to explain why you are so socially inept. And somehow it makes her laugh. It wasn't what you were going for, but you'll take it. Don't blow it.

A first impression is its own story, an immediate perception, conveyed in a moment. And the lesson, the point of it, it lasts. That very lesson informs your worldview, it's so powerful. It represents a level of truth – this idea, in all its nuance. It's a full story told with a beginning, a middle and an end. We all participate in it, whether we're the character in someone else's story that they build in the moment, or whether we are the narrator formulating it for ourselves. And we're populating it with all the people and things we see, and ascribing meaning to them through all the subtle or not so subtle things they do.

I think of the buildup between two ancient armies assembled for battle at dawn. As both armies form their ranks, one side perceives the other. They size each other up. One side marches in unison, its soldiers' armor brilliant and clean, forged in the best kilns. Their movements are crisp, their maneuvers smooth like water. When they move, it's with fluidity, effortless, they don't crash. They are uniform and they are well trained. You can pick out the different units within the ranks – the archers stand behind the main force, the cavalry forms on a ridge off to a flank. The spears and shields of the infantry form a blockade against anyone who would dare try to break through. Their short swords clang in unison against their shields, creating a metallic clanging that echoes through the canyons surrounding the battlefield. They're professional. Their war cries are intimidating, they chant in unison. This is no hoard of peasant rabble. These are professional warriors committed to one end – death.

And this is that first impression – the other side sees the presentation. They see it and they're struck with a sense of dread. In that moment, they've already lost the battle, before the first arrow has even been fired, before the first order has even been made to initiate the charge. It's the story they've formed in their subconscious of how powerful an army they are about to face actually is. They've trained, they've assembled, and they've shown up ready to fight. A beginning, a middle, and a soon to be end.

It happens everywhere. People size each other up. In sports arenas, in the boardroom, at school, at the bar, wherever it is that people meet people, these stories play out, these first impressions. Sometimes they're built up and the anticipation drives the tension and provides time for that story to develop, kind of like the armies. Other times it's sprung on you like an ambush, real shock and awe. And the story that plays out involves you struggling to regain some ground and to salvage what you can of that very story, trying your best to take control of the role you're playing as a character in theirs. Like the situation with the girl at the bar, where suddenly you're her romantic clown for the evening.

Police work is almost all first impressions – sizing people up, forming an opinion, developing a story. It's constantly meeting new people, starting conversations, exercising your socializing muscles. Figure the person out, figure out the story, and then work the problem. The question you're almost always asking, is "What's this guy's deal?"

A first impression, a story, a kernel of truth. That's Chico Fire.

The first time I met Chico Fire, he told me he wanted to suck my dick.

He flattened his hand like he was about to do a karate chop, then got this drunken googly eyed look and put his hand up to his throat, just below his Adam's apple and tilted his head back slightly.

"All the way down to here, motherfucker!"

"Jesus Christ, drive!"

I was on patrol with Dan the first time I met Chico Fire. I was fairly new to the unit and Dan was giving me the local tour.

"You ever meet Chico Fire?"

"Who's Chico Fire?"

We drove around for a bit, all the while keeping an eye out for Chico, even though I didn't know who or what Chico was.

Dan showed me where on one corner I could usually find someone slinging rock, whereas on another corner I could usually find someone slinging heroin. Then about halfway down another block by a particular grouping of tents, you could pretty reliably score some meth if you were looking for it. The ecosystem, order without order, a place for everything.

And then we found Chico Fire.

Chico Fire was hanging out with about three other people next to a couple of cars parallel parked near 5th and Towne. They were carrying on, joking, having a time. As we rolled up, I could see them quickly try to hide their beers. But we weren't there for enforcement – this was an educational moment.

Dan tells me, "Watch this, he's gonna say some crazy shit to you, just watch." He calls out from the driver side, "Hey Chico, that you?"

"Heyyyyy!" Chico replies as he saunters over to the car.

Chico Fire is wearing tight black jeans with a long pocket wallet chain on his right side, black combat boots, and a halter top which exposes his portly gut. He's also wearing thick framed, dark colored glasses. They give him some age and paint a caricature of sophistication – street sophistication. Chico has been around the block a time or two in his day, and he's got the wrinkles to prove it. There's also a subtle aura of crazy about him, like he's a wise Skid Row mage, tapping into a deeper wisdom of the neighborhood. He most definitely fits in. Like a Skid Row Jedi.

"What's up, Chico?"

Chico looks me up and down. I'm sitting in the passenger seat and he's right outside my window. He bends down to eye level with us and leans in, placing his forearms on the car door.

"I don't think I met you before, you new out here?"

"I been at Central for awhile. New to the unit though," I say.

"Ok because I never met you before, I know all these guys who work Safer Cities. How you doing, Danny?"

"I'm good Chico."

"Yeah, I'm new to Safer Cities."

Chico is all smiles, seems genuinely friendly. He's obviously on a first name basis with my partner. To us he's Dan, but to Chico he's Danny. I'm starting to get the picture. Chico Fire.

I ask Chico, "So my partner says they call you Chico Fire? Is that your real name?"

Chico laughs, "Yes that's my real name."

49

I reply, "Bullshit, that's what's on your license? I don't believe it."

Chico laughs again as he reaches for his wallet. He pulls out his license and shows it to me. Wasn't lying, plain as day on an official California state ID, Chico Fire.

I let out a chuckle, "Crazy! Was that the name you were born with or did you legally change it to that?"

Smiling, "It's my birth name."

"It's just so smooth, like it has a natural ring to it, Chico Fire. Like how some people are given names as a baby that they could only ever grow up to be a ball player, you know?"

Chico nods as he puts his license back in his wallet. "Birth name, right there. Always been a conversation starter, I've leaned into it, as you can see."

Chico steps back and does a twirl for us, displaying his wondrous figure.

Dan asks, "So where you been, Chico? I haven't seen you out here in a while."

Chico shrugs his shoulders and leans back in towards the car. "Oh, I got picked up for a sales case, I was slingin' a little cavi. Simple shit." Note: Cavi is street vernacular for crack cocaine.

Dan replies, "But you're out now, that's good. You done with the case?"

"Released on parole, you know how it is."

"How's it being back in the neighborhood?"

"It's good, but you know, it ain't like it used to be out here."

"What do you mean by that, Chico?"

I can sense things starting to take a turn. Chico and I haven't met before, it's all first impressions here. I'm sizing

50

him up, he's sizing me up. We're each trying to get a gauge on the other's limits. And everything's going into it, not just listening to the words, but reading the body language, the subtle clues, the subtle hints that push you in a direction one way or the other. And it isn't just with me, it's the totality of the scenario. Dan is trying to coax something out of Chico. I can't tell exactly what it is, but Chico is picking up on it. He can't be too careful, so he's thinking about testing the waters. He's getting closer and closer.

"Well you know, you used to be able to come out here and hang out and party. It's just not what it used to be, out here on Skid Row."

"What do you mean, to party?" asks Dan.

"You know, like to have a good time."

"What do you mean, to have a good time?"

"You know, like –

Chico looks left, then right, then at me as if to size me up one last time, then back at Dan. "You know, like to come down here and eat ass and suck dick!"

Chico rolls his shoulders violently to emphasize how much he is into the idea of eating ass and sucking dick.

Dan feigns surprise, "Really Chico?! You used to do that?"

I call out to Jesus, yelling "Jesus!"

"Back when you could, yeah! Still do when I can!"

"When's the last time you did something like that?"

"Shit…when I went to court, there was this handsome police officer, a Mexican man. His penis was down to his *knees* almost, I could just imagine seeing it through his pants!"

Then Chico looks at me, "Kinda like you, if you weren't in uniform, I'd have you all the way down to here!"

Then he does the karate chop thing on his throat.

"You're handsome too, all you Mexican policemen are, you Latinos. Are you Mexican?"

I edge away from the door and yell at Dan, "Jesus Christ, drive!"

As Dan peels out down the road, he erupts in laughter. I look back and see Chico laughing wildly, getting smaller and smaller as we drive away. Dan's laughter dies down as we turn the corner, and he says, "Now you've met Chico Fire, what'd you think? Hell of a first impression, huh?"

*   *   *

"Zoo's closing, time for you animals get the fuck up outta here!"

Like clockwork, as soon as she'd see the black and whites pull up and park along the ten-foot-high wrought iron gates, you could be sure to see Chukums taking charge of her park.

"You ain't gotta go home, but y'all niggas need to get the fuck out the park!"

Chukums was like the unofficial mayor of San Julian Park, a neighborhood staple. She wasn't even a heavy hitter like some of the Grape Streeters who would post up and have their lookouts scattered throughout the area, all operating in the dope game like a dysfunctional beehive or something of the like. No, Chukums was just that motherfucker nobody wanted to cross, not the police, not the gangsters. With some people you just know better.

Somehow the responsibility to close the park fell to our unit, even though it had been agreed upon that somebody from the local outreach house would handle it. But because they were too inconsistent and we had seven-day coverage, we ended up handling it most of the time. The big issue was that at night, the parks became a hub for violent crime, so the solution...close the park, lock the gates. Of course, it wasn't a fool proof solution – after all, people could just scale the gates, but it was enough of an obstacle to be inconvenient enough to discourage people from going in.

Chukums was always posted up near one of the three wide entrances by the gate. She was homeless and lived on the streets, and she had a glass eye and a limp. She was always drunk. She was always angry. She usually had a titty out, just didn't give two halves of a damn. A real motherfucker, that Chukums.

And she had jokes.

One she told us while we were finishing up closing the park. We were walking back towards our cars, it was me, Gina, this guy Phil who was a short, happy go lucky former Marine, and his partner Sabrina, one of our other senior coppers in the unit. We had to pass Chukums, who had made her way back to her spot and was posted up on the sidewalk. She didn't really have a full-on tent exactly, it was more of a stack of suitcases and a broken chair or two with a tarp draped over it, covering her belongings. She's standing up going through her things, getting ready to settle in for the night.

She turns to us, "Zoo's closed officers, time to go home."

"You know we're just starting out, we'll be out here til at least three when the other shift comes through, you know how we do," I reply.

She smiles at us as we approach, it's mischievous.

"Hey, I heard a new joke. You guys wanna hear it?"

"What you got Chukums."

She burps. She's definitely been drinking all damn day, it's a miracle she can still stand up. She's not standing straight, doing more of a side-to-side sway, in the only way someone with a natural limp could somehow look like they're even more off balance.

She starts into the joke, "This one's about two hoes, one's named Britney, the other's named Cindy. Now Britney, she *real* good at sucking dick. Cindy, not so much. So one day they meet up with a trick, and they go to the hotel and he tells em what he wants. So Britney, she go down on him, and she starts suckin' and suckin' and suckin' and she doin' it real good..."

Chukums mimes sucking a dick.

"She play wit his nuts, uses both hands, goes all the way back, she does real good."

She keeps miming it. It's grotesque, Chukums is opening her mouth, both hands wrapped around an imaginary penis, making gagging noises interspersed with burps. She's moving around, swaying back and forth, somehow not tumbling head over ass. Sabrina is standing closest to her and has a look on her face that is just beyond reality. There's really no better way to describe her look than the look you would get if you were, well, standing next to a drunken, belligerent homeless woman jokingly miming the act of sucking a penis while reeking of alcohol.

54

"Next it's Cindy's turn. She gets down on her knees and starts suckin' but she got big ass buck teeth like a beaver, and she tries suckin' it and he goes AHHHHHH!!! She's all fucked up, she's all teeth."

We start laughing. Chukums is *really* getting into the story. Sabrina lets escape a nervous smile, lost in the surreal moment of the insanity, the unofficial mayor of San Julian Park, a real motherfucker that Chukums, telling her a blow-job joke.

"So the trick gets mad and tells her to stop. The three of em, they go to meet up with the pimp, and the trick says to the pimp, I want a refund. The pimp, he says he don't do refunds, but asks what's the problem with his bitches. The trick, he pulls out his dick and says see for yourself. And he says to the hoes, show him what you done to me. Now Britney, she gets down like before and starts doing it again, and she does him up real good. The pimp, he says that's right, that's how she do, what's the problem? Then Cindy, she gets down, and again, she's all teeth."

We stifle our laughs, not sure where she's going with this.

"So the pimp gets real quiet, and I mean *real* quiet and looks real serious at the trick, then looks at Britney, then looks at Cindy. And all of a sudden he yells BITCH!!!"

Chukums yells "BITCH!!!" directly in Sabrina's face, you can literally see the moisture from her breath. If alcohol breath had a color you could actually see the smell itself.

"BITCH!!! I swear, if I have to show you this shit one more goddamn time!"

Chukums pauses –

"And then the pimp gets down on his knees and starts blowing the trick!"

We die laughing. Chukums loses her cool and breaks from the joke, "That's not it! So the pimp finishes suckin' his dick, and when he stands up and wipes his mouth, then the trick looks at him and says, ok I don't want my money back this time. But next time I come looking for some ass, you don't send me these busted ass hoes. You come down here your damn self! Hah!"

Chukums breaks down laughing and shuffles away, waving her hand in the air with her back towards us as she departs her sidewalk stage, like she just did a mic drop.

We all look at each other, baffled. Did she just do a bit for us? Like a standup bit? Then we look at Sabrina, who is laughing but still in shock.

Sabrina says the first words through laughter, "What the hell just happened?"

Phil replies, "That joke was hilarious!"

In reality, I don't remember what we found more entertaining, the joke itself, the delivery, or the fact that Chukums had just straight up seemingly called Sabrina a bitch loud and directly to her face.

That wasn't the last of Chukums' jokes. It became sort of a regular thing after that, we'd be closing the park or responding to a call, and of course she would be in one of her usual spots, and every time we'd see her we'd ask, "Hey Chukums, you got any jokes today?"

Sometimes she would have something, other times she would be in a mood, either too drunk or just got in a fight. You know, just having finished dealing with some street shit.

It's a rough neighborhood and it doesn't always treat its residents kindly, not even the de facto mayor.

Here's another one Chukums threw our way. What do you call a bunch of Mexicans in a mosh pit? Bean dip. Not every joke was a winner – usually they were just plain racist. But I guess it's all about personality and delivery, and *those* she had.

One time she tells us one of these jokes, we laugh at it, not her best but we don't want her to take it too rough. She tells us it's her birthday the next day. We ask how old she is, and charming woman that she is tells us, "You motherfuckers can just look up my birthday." That's Chukums.

We ask her when the last time she's really celebrated her birthday, or if anyone out here actually does anything nice for her. She grows a little more reserved, her gaze a little deeper, like her one good eye is looking backwards towards better times.

"I don't celebrate no more, it's not like that out here."

"Well that's too bad, no reason nobody should at least wish you a happy birthday on your birthday."

"Well, that's mighty kind of you two, but you better get going cuz I got shit to do. Bean dip, hahah!"

She turns and walks away. We go our way and that's the end of it.

Gina and I are working together and it's the day after Chukums told us her bean dip joke. It's her birthday. Right out the gate we beeline straight for Sprinkles on south Figueroa, narrowly missing getting roped into another masturbation caper. We buy a red velvet cupcake, the fanciest one they have, with cream cheese frosting applied to look like flower petals, glittery sprinkles and a sparkling water.

We make our way back towards San Julian and track down Chukums.

When we pop out the car, she looks up from her spot. She doesn't seem too chipper – in fact she seems more drunk than usual, with a nice side of attitude and belligerence to go with it. With some people that energy just radiates from them, can't escape it. Gina gets out the car with the paper bag and approaches her.

"See, we didn't forget. Told you we'd remember your birthday."

She pulls out the cupcake in the plastic to-go container and hands it to Chukums, who takes it with what at first is hesitance, suspicion even. It's like something inside her was so damaged that even the simple act of receiving a gift was enough to put her on the defensive.

Then Gina takes out the plastic fork and seltzer water and hands them both to her. "We can't stay long because we're holding calls, but those are for you."

Slowly someone we'd never seen starts to emerge from behind that cold exterior of drunken anger, that front facing bitterness towards the world. She doesn't completely transform, that wouldn't even be possible at this point and there's something in her look that inherently knows this. She knows that she is who she is, and that person is beyond repair. But the faint hint of that other person knows it, and it comes out for just a moment, fleeting as it may be.

"Happy birthday, Chukums. Thanks for telling us awesome jokes, people need that out here," I say. "You have a happy birthday and enjoy the cupcake, it's a good one."

She smiles and sees us off, not saying anything. We make our way down San Julian and pick up a call, on to the next one. As we're driving, Gina reads off the comments of the call. Not much else to say. In the car, a shared silence, a shrug of understanding. Like it or not, Chukums was as much a part of the tapestry of our lives as we were of hers.

Looking back, it very well may have been the nicest thing someone had done for her in years. There's no way of knowing for sure because I only know the look she had when she realized she wasn't being scammed, but rather was the second party to an act of common decency and camaraderie from what almost amounted to a work colleague. It's something we take for granted, the ability to connect with others. When your coworkers bring you a cake on your birthday or tell the waitstaff at a restaurant to bring you a dessert and to come sing to you, it's so easy to write it off as an embarrassing tease. But the reality is at least somebody is thinking of you. When that hasn't happened in a while, when you can't remember the last time you engaged with someone in simple honesty, when all you've had is loneliness and struggle, a simple gesture that may seem like it means so little can mean so much. It's all about perspective.

*   *   *

When we tell stories, we naturally include parts of ourselves in them. Whether specifically as a main character experiencing it, tangentially as someone who witnessed it, or even manifested as a sort of proxy for our own version.

I can't help but think to that one joke she told us, the one with Britney and Cindy. On some level after she told us that joke, it's almost like as she was walking away, she left us with the suspicion that maybe she was one of the characters in the story. Was she Britney? Was she Cindy? Was she really both of them? It wouldn't be a far cry from reality that maybe she was one of those two way back when and the street life just got to her, finally broke her, and this is where she ended up. One too many beatdowns, one too many gangbangs, one too many rapes or fights or robberies and she ended up at the corner of 5th and San Julian. She wouldn't be the first and she won't be the last. That's where they all end up, at least in spirit.

And that's where her story is lost. A person only truly dies when nobody is left to tell their story. The tragedy of someone like Chukums is that she is destined to be forgotten, living on only as a character in an experience like this, but as soon as she slips from my mind, there's no other way to mark it, there's no other way to memorialize it. She has nobody out there to remember her, that much is evident.

As for us, there's no crime, there's no report, there's no record. Just like the thumb in the ass guy whose name I can't remember. I remember it all, I remember him, but that's it. There's no report that goes with that caper. It was just a felony rev warrant – all that means is he was supposed to check in with his parole officer, for whatever reason didn't, and the parole officer put in the paperwork to have his parole revoked. Bring him back for the original crime he committed, nothing new, no new storytelling element to it. Unless there was something notable with us bringing him in, like a foot pursuit or a use of force or he needed serious medical care or something that would otherwise expose the city to major liability, it's not a story worth telling, at least in the eyes of the city. The only actual record of that interaction is a small logline in our daily activities report, something that might read close to "Ped stop for indecent exposure investigation, booked parolee for felony warrant suspect at MDC jail." But so much is lost, save for this retelling, or the oral retelling at 3am in a parking lot with friends.

It speaks to the true power of storytelling, the ability to continue someone or something's existence when it would otherwise end, simply for the sake of the story. There may be some inherent truth to that simple notion. Evolutionary biologists would argue that the purpose of life is to continue for the sake of life itself, to pass on the genes, to propagate the DNA, to reproduce. Its roots come on the heels of the theory that the reason we are here and the reason we are the way that we are is because we evolved to be that way – that weaker versions of ourselves with weaker traits not as conducive to survival gradually died out, paving the way to what we are in the present. By this thinking, purpose itself is to evolve – it's the greatest evolutionary shrug you can reason towards. There's some element of truth to it because it feels like a letdown. It's so anticlimactic, that we are simply the results of cosmic and evolutionary happenstance – because so often it *feels* like there's more to it.

In a story that takes this same form, the shrug comes about and seems to reveal so much truth because there's a resigned understanding that there's no greater purpose to it, that it simply is what it is. Not much else to say but to get on with it. And that's how we tell stories. Discuss it if it makes sense, write about it if it is worth writing about, memorialize it if you need to, retell it if it's worth retelling. If you don't do it, then the story gets lost.

The truth is that there is tragedy in the fact that most stories *are* lost to time, relegated to their own 5th and San

Julians. Here, these stories represent shadows of our past selves, existing and not existing, being remembered and then forgotten. If we're lucky, maybe they'll be memorialized by someone like Chukums, who will tell them to a cop who decides to turn it into a joke instead of just moving on to the next call.

As for Chico Fire? I don't know what greater truth could possibly be gleaned from that one. I may just not have the level of requisite wisdom to figure it out. I'm no street Jedi, so better to just drive away terrified than risk the karate chop. Hell of a first impression, hell of a lasting impression.

Discovering Influences

When I was about fifteen years old, I saw a performance that would, unbeknownst to me, define a good portion of my adult life. That defining content was the first season of Chappelle's Show, and I first saw it with my parents. Growing up, my parents never hesitated to expose my brothers and me to popular content; there was real value in introducing us at early ages to cultural icons, exposing us to the minds that shaped the world and influenced how we all experienced it. It was an interesting parenting choice – how much of it was intentional I'll never be sure, so I'll just chalk it up to good instincts. My family was close enough and had open and honest enough communications that they were able to expose us to content, gauge its level of appropriateness, intuit how we were interpreting it, and guide us through the experience.

Part of that guidance was the real-life stories that usually accompanied the topic, whether it was the coming-of-age type shenanigans of my dad and his cousins growing up in New York City during the disco and Rick James eras, or like how on mom's side of the family we definitely had some characters who towed the line of being black white supremacists, a la Clayton Bigsby. It's both hilarious and shocking when you see it on television because fiction has a strange way of mimicking reality. In this regard, the storytelling provides the context and through that, the guidance.

My parents learned pretty quickly that I was mature enough to experience content that nowadays most parents wouldn't even think of showing their teenage children. At the age of fifteen, my dad introduced me to Taxi Driver. He told me it was a classic from the seventies, one of the defining movies of the era. And it hit with the relevance of a higher wisdom which still resonates today and is arguably more relevant forty years later than it was when it was first released. The sheer power of the filmmaking was something unlike I had ever seen before. That was my first exposure to Martin Scorsese, and it paved the way in defining how I viewed the power of film, and more specifically, the art of storytelling. I thank my father for that one.

From there I would go on to seek out movies not just for their entertainment value, but to be able to experience and interpret them for their artistic merit as well. I discovered that this type of storytelling had the potential to provide greater insights into the human condition – a greater glimpse at truth, told through a visual medium. Through high school and college, I saw all the old and new classics – from the likes of The Godfather, Raging Bull, Schindler's List, Yojimbo and 12 Angry Men, all the way through Pulp Fiction, Silence of the Lambs, and No Country For Old Men. And it wasn't just the movies – through my mother I discovered The Beatles, The Rolling Stones, Queen and Frank

Sinatra. My father gave me his copy of Shogun from the bookshelf and helped me discover jazz greats like Miles Davis and Charlie Parker.

The thing both my parents really killed it in was comedy. And for both of them, whose formative years were spent back in the early and mid-eighties, Eddie Murphy was comedy's king. I remember sitting up late at night watching reruns of Saturday Night Live sketches where Eddie Murphy did an impression of Buckwheat from the Little Rascals and claimed to be the fifth Beatle.

My real indoctrination into the world of comedy came with one of his most famous standup specials, Delirious. I distinctly remember sitting down with both of my parents at the age of fourteen to watch Eddie Murphy's Delirious. I was blown away. The way he could command a crowd, work the room – a gigantic arena – to not miss a beat, the improv work, it was a master class in the art of standup. While dad was head over heels and doubled over laughing, mom was trying to be the adult in the room by slapping him while trying to stifle her own laughs. In their defense, it was probably a little raunchier than they had remembered. But the memory that stuck was the laughter that it wrought, and in some sense, that's the only part that really mattered.

Now that the gig was up and the damage was already done, they promptly followed up Delirious with Murphy's next special, Raw. Just as raunchy, just as masterful – I was hooked. They took me to my first live set for my sixteenth birthday. Standup comedy became a lifelong love of mine, and now it's one of the prisms through which I see the world. And at its core, what is standup beyond being the most simplified version, the purest form of storytelling? A person on a stage with a microphone, telling stories – setups and punchlines. In the many years since, I've realized that some of my favorite standup comedians are simply masterful storytellers, people who somehow manage to get at the most important part of a story and convey its truest essence possible. And the reactions are usually laughter.

What strikes me about standup is that just like all true stories, they share a commonality in their final moments. What happens when you get to the end, after the big joke of the set that brings the audience to tears, after the power closer? After you've spent the better part of an evening laughing, whether in person or at home on your couch, there's that moment – that 3am moment in the parking lot where you're just waiting for another call because all the stories have already been told, and you're just nursing that final cup. Once you leave the theater, once you close out your tab at the bar, once you turn off the tv, it finally all coalesces around that one relevant point: you laughed, and that's the absolute truth. It doesn't get any purer than that.

*   *   *

There was one sketch and character in particular on Chappelle's Show that always got me. The character was Tyrone Biggums, a local crackhead who got into crackhead adventures. He had a red skullcap, a dirty, rotten grayish brown suit, chapped, ashy skin, and white powder stains around his mouth.

Now bear in mind, I had never actually met or seen a crackhead in real life. I just thought it was funny. Little did I know that the reason my parents were laughing so hard was because they actually *knew* people like that, including some family members who had become addicted and turned into crackheads themselves. While tragic, it didn't take away from the fact that Chappelle's depiction of a typical crackhead was spot on accurate. And that reality is an absurd comedy that I would later experience first-hand in my career.

My father once told me, "You can't argue with a drunk." And he was right, or at least partially. While you can in fact argue with a drunk, you learn pretty fast that you're not accomplishing much. So functionally, you cannot argue with, have a discussion with, or reason with a drunk. But a crackhead? That's a different story altogether.

I've found that crackheads – or baseheads, as they are also commonly referred to, deriving from the fact that when cocaine is "rocked up" and formed into a solid, it is referred to as cocaine base – star in a leading role in an unusually high percentage of my experiences, and they exemplify the epitome of absurdity. It's due to what I describe as "crackhead behavior."

Crackhead behavior is distinctly different from other behaviors from the likes of drunks, meth users, or heroin addicts. As mentioned before, you can't have a conversation with a drunk, and similarly, you can't have a conversation with a meth head or heroin addict. Think about every conversation you have ever had with a drunk; they are forgetful, they repeat themselves, they piss themselves and puke everywhere, stumble down the street, and are generally insufferable unless you are also just as drunk with them.

Drunks are very easily influenced and easy to manipulate, and the alcohol impairs their judgment, so if you point them in a direction they will barrel down that path, regardless of how illogical it may be and with no consideration as to what happened just before or what will happen after. They will support you and fight you the very next minute, on a whim.

As a cop, it's absolutely impossible to manage a drunk because they are impervious to reason or discussion. When they finally come to in a few hours, they return to being normal, and all it really takes is a few hours of sleep for the effects to wear off and for them to come to their senses.

Heroin addicts are easy enough to deal with and are generally harmless. Once they are on the nod, they are numb to the world, and their general attitude is the same. They just want to shoot up and dip out. Such is the nature of opiates.

Meth? Different story. Trying to deal with a meth head is a nightmare because the effects are so long lasting. The effects of one hit of meth will generally linger for anywhere from three to five days, and the symptoms only get worse with time. Usually when someone is tweaking – this is the term for when they are at their most intense point of the meth's influence – they experience severe paranoia and everything is elevated – heart rate, respiration, alertness – it's all elevated except their attention span, which drops severely. Dealing with someone who is tweaking is impossible. You try and explain something and they can't sit still, they can't pay attention. The paranoia gets particularly irritating because they think they are hearing and seeing things that are not actually there.

"What was that? Somebody is outside!"
"We just looked outside, there's nobody there."
"You sure, officer? I just heard em!"
"Nobody is outside, it's the wind."

"No, I saw somebody!"

"You didn't see any goddamn body!"

"I swear, I did! There it is again!"

"It's shadows from the wind and the bushes outside, there's nobody there! Stop calling us!"

It's damn near impossible to deal with somebody like this, and to try offering rational explanations to someone who cannot pay attention to assuage irrational fears is a frustrating task, to say the least.

But crack is different. A crackhead once explained to me that the reason smoking crack is so much better than powder cocaine is because the effects are so much more euphoric and immediate. When you snort a line of coke, it takes a few minutes before you feel the high. It has to work its way into your bloodstream and work its way to your brain. When you smoke it, the vapors go directly to your brain and the effect is instantaneous. The effects of one hit will only last maybe fifteen to twenty minutes, and then it wears off. And so, the nature of the crackhead is drastically different than that of the drunk, meth head, or heroin addict.

Most of the time, in between hits, crackheads are completely normal, or at least normal-ish. You can have normal conversations and discuss a variety of topics. The war in Syria? Fair game. Budget cuts to the city's services? Have at it. I have had completely informed, sober, normal conversations with crackheads about family life, my experiences on the job, their experiences and run ins with the justice system, and all manner of current events. I even once had a conversation with a guy who looked like Tyrone Biggums about how much he looked like Dave Chappelle playing Tyrone Biggums. He laughed hysterically. I've even complained with crackheads about other drug addicts and how insufferable and impossible they are to deal with. By and large, most crackheads are easy enough to pass the time with.

So what's the catch? The kicker is in the addiction itself, because it alters the crackhead's priorities. The underlying motivation for any crackhead is quite simply, to get more crack. And that informs everything they do. And when I say everything, I mean *everything*. If scoring rocks is the end goal, if that is the golden chalice, then anything is justifiable if it furthers that objective. The end will always justify the means, as long as they're getting their rocks.

Promise a crackhead a hit, and he will debase himself like no one ever has. Chappelle plays it for laughs, jokingly telling to a classroom full of kids, "And that, children, was the first time I sucked a dick for crack!" Horrible, but that's not the worst of it. I've seen a man smuggle rocks in his asshole, pull them out and get ready to smoke them, and then *immediately* shove them in his mouth because he thought he was gonna get caught and didn't want to lose them. Somebody who is that desperate for the stuff will just accept this and brush it off as just another thing, because the payoff will be that fucking worth it. Just hide em in your mouth. It defies sober logic. But to a crackhead? Makes total sense.

Crackheads will push themselves to the far extremes of physical human ability to score. There are crackheads who are hands down tougher than most Navy SEALs. As a for instance, walking back to his tent on his way to get high on some rocks he just scored, a crackhead might get hit by a car. But by God, if that isn't going to stop him from getting high.

He'll bounce right back up from the ground without missing a beat, leaving some poor motorist terrified they just killed someone. I've seen crackheads get stabbed and have their heads bashed in and outright refuse medical attention, claiming they'll just "Walk it off," as if it was just a pulled hamstring or a sprained ankle. No time for police reports, no time for medical attention. There are rocks that need smoking.

The truly baffling things are the leaps of logic crackheads make in getting themselves from situation to situation. When most people find themselves in precarious circumstances, there's usually a moment of reckoning where you take stock in the decisions you've made to get to that point, and on some level, you vow never to let it happen again. But this is a type of person who never makes that leap of self-awareness and as a result, things tend to spiral wildly out of control.

Now put yourself in the shoes of a petty criminal. You spot a car parked along the street. It's the end of the month and you're running low on cash. You're jonesing for your next score and you're a little hungry. You look left, look right, coast is clear. You walk up to the car and take a peek in the windows. Still nobody looking. You take off your sweatshirt, place it on the window, and drive an elbow straight through it, smashing the window while protecting your arm from getting shredded by the broken glass. In the center dash there is a small change cup with maybe a dollar's worth of change, a candy bar, a pair of headphones, and some kind of device, maybe it's an old mp3 player, sitting in the cupholder. Doesn't matter exactly what it is, it's shiny. What do you take?

The rational criminal would take the change – it's money, it's obvious. It can be saved and used later for a variety of things. But that's the problem. Your typical crack-head isn't thinking like a sober-minded individual. This guy needs to score *now*, he doesn't have time to save money to buy something later. He's not putting money away in a re-tirement account and hoping the interest accrues. He's try-ing to score rocks.

No, he takes the mp3 player and the headphones, and of course the candy bar. His reasoning is nobody will rob him of the mp3 player or the headphones. Of course, it doesn't occur to him that he would be the exact kind of per-son to rob someone of these particular items, but never mind that. He's gonna eat the candy bar, that will be enough to hold him out until he scores, so he won't have to worry about not eating – after all, the endorphins released from the sugar and the chocolate will be a nice quick burst of feel good.

He's gonna barter the mp3 player and headphones, or maybe he'll hang onto the headphones. Either way, he can use those as a bargaining chip when he goes to barter with the dealer. Best case, he includes the headphones with the player and scores an extra rock. Worst case, he has to give them up, and he can just break into another car if he still wants some headphones. The plan makes total sense, it's elaborate, well thought out. This is *science*. This is *crack-head science*.

The next step, he takes his stolen goods to his guy and offers to barter for the rocks. The guy inspects the mp3 player, puts it in his backpack, and hands the guy his bindle. Doesn't want the headphones, they're a shit brand. He takes the bindle and sticks it in his pocket, then does his excited "I just got my crack!" walk as he dances his way down the street with the sense of purpose only typically seen in, well, a crackhead who just scored some rocks.

And not only is he going to go smoke up – this momentous occasion calls for celebration – he's going to go hit up his side piece. She's a prostitute, for sure, but she's good to him. He pays her because it's the right thing to do, not just because she's a prostitute. After all, he's not uncivilized. And best part about it, he got to keep the headphones.

Now that he's bartered away the stolen mp3 player for the crack, and because he didn't have any money to begin with, he's going to pay the prostitute *using* the crack. They're gonna split the hit in his tent. They each smoke up a bit, get the blood flowing, and then go to town on each other in the most awful way imaginable. Just filthy conditions, it's all unsanitary, just shameful and grotesque. And at the end, she holds out her hand – time to pay up.

"Give me my rock you owe me."

"Bitch, you already smoked it, that's all I got!"

"Fuck you that was before, you owe me some rock! I didn't want to do all that, I only did it because you were gonna give me another one!"

"Don't start your shit with me, go find some more if you want some!"

"You wasn't saying all that when your dick was in my mouth, little dick motherfucker!"

"Fuck you, bitch!"

"I ate your ass!"

The arguing intensifies and she starts aggressively rummaging through his things. A mild struggle ensues, she snatches the pair of headphones from the floor, slaps him across his face, and takes off running.

Now take a moment to think about it. You are that guy, what is your next move? Your sober mind would tell you, maybe call it a night. You just got some action, smoked a rock, had a candy bar. Not a bad evening, right? Wrong. That bitch stole your headphones, she's a damn thief, and damned if you're going to take this lying down and accept being a victim. Time to call the police, because you've been robbed.

Scenarios just like this play out more often than is sensible to admit, and is the perfect example of how crackhead behavior just spirals towards insanity. Every decision that was made was in the furtherance of going deeper and deeper into this bizarre world, where crack rules, and the unrelenting pursuit of it is king.

The funny thing is that more likely than not, that prostitute who ran off with the headphones will make her way to the police station to file a rape report, because in her crack addled mind, she never actually wanted to do any of those things. She didn't *want* to eat ass. She only did it for the crack. And since he didn't want to give her the crack she thought she was entitled to, she never technically consented to anything. Kind of. So, in her mind, she has *kind of* been raped. Maybe? At the very least, she feels he did her wrong, and he needs to get his comeuppance. Especially after all that filthy shit he did to her. The officer reluctantly takes the report, because it's not worth catching a complaint over – refusing to take a report from a citizen reporting a crime. Even though in his heart of hearts, he knows it's just a business deal gone wrong.

What all this results in is two reports sitting on a couple detectives' desks – one for robbery and one for rape, with each listing the other's victim as the suspect. Each detective goes through the motions, does the follow-ups and submits both cases. Maybe there is video corroborating the account of the robbery, or an eye witness who saw her take something from the guy and run off. Maybe that same witness heard what sounded like a rape happening in the tent, because it was just that obscene and disturbing. But there's no way to definitively say what happened, just one of those capers. Not a chance on this one. Ultimately, both cases get dropped because when you boil it down, it's nothing more than a crackhead caper, just all kinds of ridiculous. Everyone spinning their wheels and chasing ghosts, trying to sort out crimes that may or may not have happened. And the strangest part of it all? The guy whose car got broken into in the first place – never even bothered to make a report. The headphones, after all, were just a shit brand anyway.

On Absurdity

"Santiago, you really are a goddamn magnet."

"Sorry."

My partner for the night, Dan, sits there with about five separate reports scattered across his workstation. We're already about thirty minutes overtime and haven't even started the pre-booking paperwork. How we got roped into this one, somehow it's my fault. I have a history of attracting the most mind-boggling capers that are damn near impossible to explain to a supervisor demanding to know why we're going to be four hours over. This was one of those "it literally fell into our lap" kinds of things. But because it's me, it should have been expected.

Rewind about an hour and a half. It's about 2am, we're on the final stretch. We're off in an hour, it's been a quiet second half of the night. We did some decent work early on, cut a few tickets, made some good stops, made life a little more difficult for the gangsters and dealers in the area, call it a success. But this is that witching hour, when it's most dangerous to venture out. Dangerous, not in terms of physical danger – that's pretty consistent no matter the time. No, it's dangerous in terms of the risk of having to do actual *work*. Nobody likes getting involved in a crazy scheme where you really need to rack your brain when you're in hour nine of a ten-hour shift. If you're cruising around, the universe has a strange way of sending you the craziest thing it can gin up at the most inconvenient times. While good police instinct at this point would be to hang out on the roof and listen out for any emergency backup calls or hot shots, I'm bored and want to drive a few laps around the border of the division to pass the time before we pack it up and bring it in.

We drive down Wall St, past Winston for about the fourth time in the last half hour. Same few transients sleeping in the same spots, haven't moved, probably won't be moving for another few hours til when the sun starts to rise. We've seen our same Skid Row bird that always hangs out at the intersection. We can't be sure the exact breed, it has a spear-like beak that it uses to skewer rats, usually a pretty gnarly scene to witness. It's kind of like a pelican, but not as big. It's just ghetto, another product of the area. Definitely not native to Skid Row, but like everyone else who ended up there, it's just been institutionalized, another part of the streets.

We turn down Boyd, a one-way street. Final lap. We're not finding anything else tonight, radio's quiet, it's dead out. We're about halfway down the block when I notice a beam of light coming up Wall – probably another black and white, we've been passing each other for the last two hours. Everybody's bored.

But then the beam gets erratic, followed by the screeching of tires, and low and behold, it's not a black and white that comes barreling around the corner right at us, but a white cargo van. Coming down Boyd, a one-way, about to pop us right in our kisser. Dan flips on the lights, I jerk towards the right hoping to avoid a head on collision and lean on the horn, and the cargo van slams on its brakes and comes to a stop about six feet from us.

"The fuck are you doing, it's a one way!"

"I'm sorry officers, don't mind me, that's my mistake!"

The lady driving the van is a heavyset black woman. Her hair is wild, hasn't been combed in weeks, and her eyes are buggy, probably hasn't slept in weeks.

I yell back at her, "Why you driving so damn fast, you almost killed us!"

"I'm sorry, I swear I'm sorry, I'm in a rush, I got diarrhea I'm about to shit my pants, I'm trying to get home!"

She keeps stammering. Does she really have to shit? Who knows, we don't care enough to find out.

"Well slow down and pay attention, you're gonna kill somebody driving like a goddamn maniac," I reply.

I put the car in drive as she continues stammering, obviously trying to manically talk her way out of a ticket. She's definitely out here capering, but at this hour everyone's out here capering. No obvious crime, off in an hour, not worth the trouble.

Then suddenly all that changes.

"Help me, help me! She kidnap me!"

A skinny Asian guy pops up out of nowhere in the passenger seat like a goddamn jack-in-the-box. "Help me officers!"

The lady turns and backhands him across the chest, "Shut up Jimmy, sit down!"

"She kidnap me, she kidnap me!"

"Sit down and shut up Jimmy, what's wrong with you?!" She hits Jimmy again and tries to push him back down. "He's fine officers, he's just kidding, he's fine," then back at Jimmy, "I said sit your ass down, I'm gonna shit everywhere!"

"Help meeeee!"

I turn to Dan and his look says it all. He lowers his head and mutters, "Only with you, dude. You had to take that last lap."

"Never fucking fails," I reply. I'm really earning my nickname this time, I'm definitely the shit magnet of the unit.

I put the car back in park. I guess we're doing this.

"Alright lady, step out of the car," I say as I close my door behind me. Dan gets out on his side and approaches the van.

The Asian guy, "Thank you thank you! She crazy!"

The lady, "Shut up Jimmy! Officers please, I swear everything's ok, he's fine!"

She keeps pleading as I make my way over to the passenger side while Dan approaches her in the driver seat. As he's opening the door to have her step out of the van, she continues pleading. Everything's ok, Jimmy's fine, they know each other, she has diarrhea and is about to shit herself, yada yada yada.

I open the passenger side door and Jimmy starts spouting off a bunch of what I can only interpret as thank you's, because he's babbling on in Chinese. For some reason he's wearing nothing but tighty whities, because of course he is.

"Where are your clothes?" I demand. "What's going on here, are you being kidnapped? Why does she know your name? What is happening?"

Jimmy has apparently exhausted the extent of his English. He starts reaching for a pile of clothes sitting behind the passenger seat and starts nervously putting them on, all the while ranting in Chinese. Why these capers always involve people not wearing clothes I'll never know. When I first came on the job, I had no idea police work would involve this much nudity, and never the good kind.

The quick summary for this story is that after requesting a supervisor and another two units to assist, we finally manage to find a Chinese translator to tell us Jimmy's side of the story. He knows this lady as a previous acquaintance – translate, he pays her for sex and they smoke crack together, not necessarily in that order. Jimmy owns the van. He works at the fish market not too far from where we are. He picked her up to give her a ride – translate, she was going to *take* a ride – but first she has to stop and pick up some beer at the liquor store. She goes into the store while Jimmy waits in the van.

Moments later she comes sprinting out the store and jumps in. Jimmy, with his limited English, panics and doesn't grasp that she wants him to push the accelerator down to the floor to get them the hell out of there, so she physically grabs him and tosses him aside – she's easily two hundred forty pounds, Jimmy is maybe a buck twenty – and hops in the driver seat herself.

She takes off, speeding through the streets of downtown until they make their way up to where we encounter them. Jimmy, of course is terrified because she's pushing seventy on surface streets and he doesn't know where she's going, driving down one-ways and the like. Why he is down to his underwear is still unclear, but he says she made him undress so he couldn't get away. Obviously.

It also doesn't explain why Jimmy has a couple crack pipes and multiple $20 rocks in his pants pockets. None of it adds up, doesn't make any sense – sometimes you just move past it. Meanwhile our girl, she never actually had diarrhea. But she did have two felony warrants, which took forever to figure out because she thought it was a good idea to lie about her name and birthday.

Her story is somehow consistent with Jimmy's and makes zero sense. The reason she came running out the store is she went in there to buy some crack from a guy but got robbed – again, makes no sense why she would be the one running away like *she's* the one who just robbed somebody, but again, sometimes you just gotta move past it. We take her for the warrants and kidnapping, we take Jimmy for possession, and we impound the van. A fitting ending to an absurd caper – just another night downtown.

My first true introduction to this level of madness came with a radio call when I had about one year on the job. In that time, sure I had been involved in some pretty wild capers including a possible mass shooter response, a handful of use of forces, vehicle and foot pursuits, and countless other capers that at this point all blend together. But this one was the first that sticks out in my mind as an example of the truly absurd.

In true Central fashion, no fewer than five radio calls came out seemingly all at once and in no particular order, of a robbery in progress, an attempted carjacking, a sexual assault in progress, a fight and a petty theft. Descriptions of all the various players in this magnificent opera included a man with a braided beard and wearing a purple Lakers jersey, a homeless guy, an overweight Russian truck driver, and a man, or maybe a woman, but more likely a man dressed as a woman, wearing a leopard print cocktail dress and purple hair.

I'm working with a guy named Rob, and while driving to the intersection we're trying to wrap our heads around what it is exactly that we're rushing into. And we're drawing blanks, can't make heads or tails of it. It all seems so disparate, no rhyme or reason as to how any of it is related.

"What do you think?"

"I don't know, maybe the purple jersey or the leopard dress will stand out, we'll see in a minute."

Our instincts prove correct, and we spot the guy in the purple jersey walking away. We pop out of the car, and he's not stopping for us. When he turns towards our direction, he's got his hands clenched in fists and he's on the balls of his feet, seems ready to fight.

At first you try to be professional, you say in an assertive voice, "Hey, step against the wall and put your hands behind your back." That's what we call "command presence." You really need to learn how to wield your command presence if you want anybody to listen to you. When command presence fails, you switch to using "tactical language," in the hopes it will de-escalate the situation and show the recipient of said tactical language that you are indeed serious about your demands. It's not a technique which is taught at the academy – in fact, in the years since I initially learned about it, it's been adopted by the department as the basis for personnel complaints for officers who do not deploy said tactical language properly – translate, getting a complaint for "Discourtesy."

Rather than learn it as an approved technique, you generally learn it from your training officer the first time somebody doesn't want to go along with the program, and so he shows you how to get it done properly. "Sir, step against the wall and place your hands behind your back!" suddenly shifts to "Motherfucker, try me! Turn around and put your fucking hands behind your back, cocksucker!" Calling someone a cocksucker to their face generally doesn't play well on camera.

Our tactical language is effective and the guy complies, albeit with a little back sass and side lip. Meanwhile other units are showing up and detaining anybody who seems to be involved, and it's easily becoming more and more chaotic by the minute.

Two officers appear to be having a standing Jiu Jitsu match with the transient across the street, desperately trying to tie his arms up to get him in handcuffs – and he looks dirty, like he really looks it. Gotta imagine he smells it too.

The Russian guy gets detained in the middle of the intersection, and he's yelling about a he-she that stole his van. We assume that was the one in the leopard dress with the purple hair. The pieces all seem to be coming together, but still without making a damn bit of sense.

Turns out our Russian guy is the victim. How much of this is true is all up for debate, but this is what we're able to piece together. He's part of a film crew company and is driving a white cargo van full of walkie talkies down 3rd St. when he's stopped at a red light. He's on the phone with

83

somebody and looks out the window and happens to make eye contact with our guy in the purple jersey.

The guy in the jersey, turns out he's a local dope dealer, well known by the guys who work narcotics. He approaches the van and signals to the driver, who lets down his window. The two exchange a few words and the purple jersey guy suddenly slugs him in the face and grabs one of the walkie talkies from the guy's lap. He starts walking away.

Our Russian, not to be taken for a bitch, gets out of the van which he leaves at the stop light and starts walking after the jersey guy. The two begin throwing fists at each other. Meanwhile, the homeless guy sees the van door is open and decides he might as well start rifling through the van for any valuables. He finds the guy's cell phone, which he had dropped in the cup holder before he went to pursue the jersey guy.

Our Russian, he sees the homeless guy in his van so he abandons his fight with the jersey guy to fight the hobo instead. Hobo now has his cell phone, and the two begin battling it out in the middle of the street. As those two duke it out, jersey guy looks at a random cross-dressing man standing on the corner – not a transgender, mind you, but a straight up man dressed as a woman, wearing a purple wig and a leopard print dress, and says to him, "If you want it, take it." Our crossdresser, he takes this all to mean he's got the green light to get in the van and drive away. Keys are in the ignition already, and hell, it's basically the same thing as a gift, right? He hops in the van and takes off. Moments later, a bunch of black and whites start showing up and detaining everybody.

So now to sort through it. Put simply, the guy in the jersey punched the victim and took his walkie talkie, so that's a robbery, the taking of someone's property through force or fear. He's getting booked for that. The homeless guy, he just took the phone from an open door, so that's just like a petty theft. But the fact that he started throwing fists with the victim as he was trying to get it back, there's the force that makes that one a robbery too. The technical term for that is called an Estes Robbery and is most commonly seen as a legal standard for a shoplifting case which escalated because the person doing the shoplifting decided they wanted to fight their way past security when they were trying to recover the merchandise. Same principle applies here. Then we have a stolen vehicle DMV report and a separate report for grand theft auto, with our Russian guy as the victim and the leopard print purple hair cross-dresser as the suspect.

Two days later, California Highway Patrol gets in a pursuit on the I10 freeway out near Palm Springs, a solid two hours east of Los Angeles. At the end of the pursuit, they detain and arrest a man dressed in a leopard print dress and wearing a purple wig. Low and behold, it's the same van, reported as stolen out of LA two days prior.

It gets crazy when the whole thing finally goes to court. The District Attorney decides to charge all three for their respective crimes as a multi-three case, which basically means all three are being charged pursuant to the same incident. Since it's all related, it's a way for defense and prosecution to streamline the process so it all stays with the same judge, and it's all handled in the same hearing and at the same trial.

The only downside is that it takes cooperation from all of the parties. By all accounts, it doesn't appear they were in cahoots together – they all just happened to be acting like independent contractors all committing a variety of crimes at the same point of opportunity.

Jersey guy and his counsel are ready to move forward, and leopard dress is ok with using the same attorney as him even though they weren't working together, but the homeless guy is a *mean* sonofabitch. He wants his *own* attorney, and doesn't want to be tried with *these* people because he don't know them motherfuckers. So he gets his own public defender, who needs time to review the case, but the other two don't want to waive their time to a hearing within ten calendar days of their arraignment like the law stipulates just because of this grouchy asshole, so now it's all kinds of fucked up.

Judge is now doing a wild juggling act trying to balance everyone's calendars and schedules while still trying to respect everyone's rights to representation and due process, and because none of them can agree on anything, a fight almost breaks out in the courtroom and the judge ends up pushing it back anyway.

Meanwhile, our victim, he works in the movie industry. He's taking time off from work to actually show up to court, which is a miracle in and of itself, for the victim to actually show up. Go figure, I didn't know you could just *not* show up to court, but apparently it happens all the time. And each time the hearing gets delayed, it's two hours paid out at time and a half for us for showing up on an off day, and a lost day of work for our victim.

After about six or seven different subpoenas, our victim finally can't take another day off just to miss work, so the case is dropped. But since this is a third strike case for the jersey guy, the DA wants this one – fast forward a few months, more subpoenas come through because the DA refiled the case. Of course, by the time this whole thing finally goes to trial, our defendants have been sitting in jail the entire time, effectively serving their sentences.

When it came time for sentencing, it all got deducted as time served, with the exception of jersey guy, who got several more years for his role in the whole matter. So in a sense yeah, justice was served, even if it meant keeping people in custody without trial for months upon months. But then again, crazier things have happened. And the little special asterisk next to this whole thing? There had been a rash of strong-arm robberies in the general area in the few months before with the suspect being described as looking just like, you guessed it, the jersey guy. In all that time he was in custody, those numbers plummeted. The justice system works in mysterious ways.

*   *   *

By now, stories like these shouldn't surprise me, but I can't help but continue to be baffled by the insanity that plays out on a daily basis.

When I was an undergraduate, I took a business law course which mainly focused on contract law – really hammered home the offer, acceptance, consideration concept. The other concept I was introduced to was the idea of something being "shocking to the conscience."

That phrase has always stuck with me. When it comes to contract law, a court will generally find a contract is valid as long as those three pillars have been met. One party makes an offer, the other party accepts the offer, and action is taken indicating that agreement is in effect – that's the consideration part.

Outside of this, to nullify a contract, an argument would have to prove there was no meeting of the minds – in other words, if both sides agreed but were way too off base and didn't realize they were agreeing to different things, then that argument can be made to nullify the contract. It's usually the result of incompetence, misrepresentation or miscommunication, sometimes all three. The only other way to really nullify a contract is if the terms of the agreement can be proven to be "shocking to the conscience." Think predatory lending, or a contract that is so unevenly lopsided that it borders on criminal.

There's something about the concept of absurdity or ridiculousness that is shocking to the conscience. Kind of like porn, it's hard to define but you know it when you see it. Something sticks out that is simply contrary to logic or sensibility, yet for whatever reason it prevails, defying every instinct or notion of propriety. Like I said, I shouldn't be baffled by the things I see anymore, but sometimes I just can't help but look at someone and say, "The fuck?"

The philosophical concept of absurdism finds its roots in the Greek myth of Sisyphus. Sisyphus was a Greek king who proved to be so crafty and deceitful during his reign that it upset the gods. After a handful of shady plays and tricks which threw the natural order of things into chaos, Sisyphus was finally dragged to the underworld. As punishment for his hubris in believing he was craftier and smarter than Zeus himself, Hades, as god of the underworld, chained Sisyphus to a massive boulder that he was ordered to roll to the top of a mountain.

But of course, there was a catch – Hades enchanted the boulder, so that when it neared the top of the mountain it would roll back down to the bottom, dragging Sisyphus with it. Therefore, the punishment was for him to forever be pushing the boulder up the mountain, an act which would prove so futile and pointless that it would frustrate Sisyphus to the end of all eternity. The myth certainly serves as a parable to warn against excessive hubris, but it also defines what forms the bedrock of the absurd – a Sisyphean task, a task that is so pointless and contrary to logic that it frustrates to no end. A task which at heart, makes your brain stop, reflect for a moment, and ask, "The fuck?"

On a deeper level, the absurd is manifested through trying to find meaning in a system that in so many ways, appears not to have any. It isn't exactly nihilism, the belief that nothing actually matters – it's more so trying to ascribe meaning where there is none. Where the nihilist would simply say there is no meaning to life, the absurdist would say the point of life is to find a point. It's this acceptance of chaos and disorder and lack of obvious meaning that drives the human condition – there has to be something greater because sometimes it *feels* like there is so much more.

It's at this point that we apply belief systems and logic to our worlds to better define them. Sometimes it happens through religion – religion ultimately provides guidelines and a context in which to discover that meaning. Others find that meaning through art or music, others find it in sex or exercise. Anything can become a religion if that's what it means to the individual. The point is that this natural human tendency, to search for truth, defines the human condition. It requires an establishment of some kind of context, which develops into culture and society, and that framework serves to establish the rules by which we all live and exist.

But what happens when what we experience flies in such stark contrast to how we have established our worldviews? What happens when the rules of sense and logic and reason that define us are challenged? It's almost like our brains reach a tipping point, *404 error, file not found.* Think about John Goodman playing Walter from The Big Lebowski, who says to Steve Buscemi's character, "Donny, this isn't 'Nam, there are rules." An unstable guy like Walter would pull a gun in a bowling alley. Others would just turn to their partners with a quizzical look. The fat black lady who kidnapped Asian Jimmy, who doesn't speak English, after a robbery of some sort, she may have diarrhea, and of course there's a bunch of crack cocaine and warrants involved. None of it makes sense, it all defies logic, and it's all evidence of the absurd.

*   *   *

Armando was a guy we ran into at 5th and San Pedro, an intersection informally and formerly known as the Cuban corner. OG Cubans from Miami, when they would get arrested back in the day for some serious level Scarface type crimes – shootings, stabbings, murder, drug trafficking, you name it – they'd get sent to prisons all over the place, and not just in Florida. Sometimes they'd catch federal cases and end up doing fifteen, twenty years.

After spending that much time in prison, you tend not to have many prospects when you get out, especially if all you really knew beforehand was crime. Word would spread amongst the Cuban population in the prison system, "When you get out, if you wanna make some money, you go to 5th and San Pedro in Los Angeles and you'll get the hook-up." They catch a one-way ticket to LA, seek out 5th and Pedro, and suddenly they're taken in by the local Cuban population – that was the only corner they owned, and the way you'd make money was through street level sales of crack cocaine.

The allure was that it was a way to work your way up to success – you start small, build the business and work your way up through the tiers, but first you gotta put in your time. Putting in the time means exactly that – putting in the time. You gotta spend time on the streets slinging. That's many an evening, many an encounter, and with more exposure comes more risk.

When all you're doing is hanging out on a corner doing hand-to-hands and trying to avoid getting jammed by the cops, it's pretty easy to fall off the straight and narrow. You might be working half the night when all of a sudden, some basehead who doesn't have enough money starts hanging around and drawing attention and because he's desperate for that fix, just won't get lost – so it forces a violent confrontation. Next thing you know you're violently assaulting someone because they're blowing up your spot, and around and around you go, and you never make any actual progress.

So there we were, Gina and I, watching Armando one June night. It isn't that it was impossible to still get a felony arrest for a narco caper after all the straight possession laws were changed to misdemeanors, it just took a little more effort because you had to piece together a sales case. A report for a sales case wasn't as simple a narrative as the suspect "Saw cop, dropped rock." For sales, you have to put in work. You need a seller, a buyer, and evidence of the sale – that's money, drugs, and people.

You start off by scoping out the scene and seeing who is out playing. After watching the scene for awhile, you recognize maybe one or two guys in particular who are hanging out on a corner on the sidewalk and never seem to leave. They're constantly looking left and right like they're keeping an eye out for the authorities, and every so often a crackhead comes up to them. They may exchange a few words, and then suddenly there's a sly little hand-to-hand transaction, and it happens *quick*, so you gotta develop an eye for it. That's the guy you're gonna watch.

You watch him for awhile. Every time somebody comes up to him, you notate the time, what the person's wearing, and what they do. If you've got a camera, photos play really well. Video plays even better. You notate every time one of these hand-to-hand transactions goes down and you witness an exchange of a small item for currency. After you witness about three or four of these, you've essentially established the person is loitering in the area for the purpose of narcotics sales – there's your probable cause to jam him for a narco investigation, you just need to be able to back up and articulate the observations which led to that determination.

At this point, you wait for a good hand-to-hand, preferably one where as the buyer is walking away, you see him put the dope in his sock or in a pants or shirt pocket. Once you know he has it and is walking away, you keep eyes on him while another unit jams him around the corner. You let that unit know to look in that particular pocket or sock, and hopefully they find the product. Once they find it, that guy gets arrested for simple possession. Then the remaining officers jam the guy who was selling and anyone else who was working with him as either a lookout or the guy holding the money or the hook – the hook is the guy who directs buyers to the guy with the product. Any of the "helpers" in the sales scheme get arrested for conspiracy to narcotics sales, and the main guy who sold the dope gets arrested for sales.

Once you bring everybody in, low and behold, you will usually recover a ton of cash, along with a good bit of individually wrapped plastic bindles containing a small rock of cocaine base. The reports tend to get pretty long and there is a lot to track, like who had what where, who recovered what, who searched who, what everyone did, so most coppers tend to shy away from it all.

Armando was one of these guys we busted for selling. Armando was a sole proprietor, was only working himself selling his individual bindles, wasn't using a hook or a money guy, so when we brought him in it was just him and the basehead our partners jammed a couple blocks away who had just bought the product.

Armando was a nice enough guy, at least for a violent drug dealer. He was a little older, in his mid-50's. He had done his time in Miami for an assortment of crimes including burglary, robbery, and narcotics sales, and he was back at it.

One of the downsides of selling out on Skid Row, again, is proximity. Plenty of customers, but you need to physically be on Skid Row. Most of these guys couldn't afford rent, so they would just pitch a tent and stay outside in the general vicinity of the corner. They'd become ingrained in the neighborhood, just another resident of the Cuban corner, a much dirtier and more degenerate version of Little Havana, with salsa music blaring and the kind of Spanish that only people from the Caribbean can understand being spoken from every mouth. Neighborhood cookouts every Saturday behind the market, the OG's playing dominoes and cards, folks trying to make an extra buck selling loose cigarettes – looseys – for a quarter apiece.

We got to chatting with Armando, and somehow the conversation turned to the general culture in the area. He recognized my accent, said I sounded different than most of the other Spanish speakers in LA. Me and this other guy I worked with named Bermudez, a Cuban guy, spoke Spanish a little differently and sounded a little off compared to the Mexican accent you typically run into in Los Angeles. Armando pegged me as being a Rican without missing a beat.

Eventually the conversation turned, like all shared cultural conversations, to food. I brought up the cookouts they are always having behind the market, he said it was great because everyone chips in and brings something, like a potluck, and they all have a good time eating and drinking and dancing and carrying on. I asked Armando what he usually brings.

In Spanish, "I usually bring the meat. I'll prepare it with some sazon and adobo, maybe some barbecue sauce, and they throw it on the grill in the back, it goes really good with the rice and beans."

"What kind of meat do you do?"

"Usually rats."

I stop dead in the conversation. "Rats?"

"Yeah, rats. They're good if you pick the right ones, you just need to skin it and clean it and put a lot of seasoning and it tastes fine, nobody says anything, people like it."

"Do they know they're eating rat meat?!"

"No, I don't tell them, I just bring the food and they take the meat, they just know it's barbecue and it tastes good."

Armando goes on to detail how he catches the rats in his tent, how he'll set out bait and catch them in traps or in a bucket, how he'll occasionally use rat poison, how he has to snap their necks if they're still alive. And once they're dead, he has to clean them off first because they're wandering around in sewage and trash, and once they're cleaned, he skins them, then rinses them again.

Then it's prep time – he'll cut up some onions, chop some garlic, throw it all in a pozole with some salt and pepper, let it stew until the meat falls off the bones.

That's usually a good dish to bring to the cookouts, a giant cauldron of rat pozole.

Or if he's not in the mood to do a pozole, sometimes he'll just skin them and douse them in barbecue sauce, season with adobo and throw them on the grill. It's no different than say prepping a Cornish hen or more closely, maybe a rabbit.

But these are rats. Skid Row rats. Not the big indigenous ones you find out in the jungles in Vietnam or South

America that the bush people eat. These are *city* rats, rats that have been scavenging in filth, scampering in the gutters amongst broken syringes and human feces and living amongst flea infested garbage. Hell, the rats are probably on drugs themselves.

I tell all this to Armando, how he's going to start a pandemic, that this is how the original plague got started back in the dark ages, because of fucking rats. But he says no way, he's not buying it. His reasoning is that he doesn't kill the small ones. When he catches those he just lets them go. He only kills the fat ones for two reasons – one is they have more meat on them so they're more worth his time to prep, and two is because since they are bigger, that means they have been around longer and therefore are likely healthier than the smaller weak ones, so they'll be safe to eat when you clean them. I'm no expert, but I don't think there's any hard science to support Armando's thesis.

Crazy thing is Armando is telling us all this and we are just staring blankly at him. It's too damn absurd to be true, he has to be pulling our leg, he's gotta be fucking with us, there's no way he's feeding rat meat to unsuspecting homeless people out there.

Or is he?

He's so serious and matter of fact and consistent with his detailing how he does it all. And after talking with him for as long as we have been, and I'm making a personal judgment here, I don't think Armando was particularly smart enough to keep the lie going for that long. He just wasn't that bright of a guy, not bright enough to keep up this charade without breaking character at least. We booked him and moved on.

If absurdity is the story that baffles the senses, then surrealism is the realization that it's all true, like a reckoning. They're like two intersecting highways of a figure eight racetrack, the absurd and the surreal – two different roads that are actually part of the same journey, just twisted and overlapping each other. And at that intersection of the absurd and the surreal, you can achieve a greater understanding, can glean some elusive truth, and hopefully find some personal fulfillment, or at the very least, catch maybe a glimpse of the truly profound, bizarre as it may be.

For us, we didn't experience the surreal part until we were executing a search warrant on a tent about three months later and happened to realize we were actually searching through Armando's tent. And low and behold, just like he had said – we almost didn't believe him at first, but like a perfectly fashioned art display, there they were: a gallon bucket, mousetraps, rat poison, a pair of tongs, barbecue sauce, a grill fork, and a couple cannisters of seasoning. He was really catching and cooking rats and feeding them to people out there.

We don't remember the evidence we found for the warrant, but bet your money we remembered the rat pozole and barbecue story – that was *our* evidence, a truly surreal realization, that Armando was telling the truth. And to our disbelief, it somehow felt profound.

OCS Shenanigans

Anyone who has ever served in the military will tell you one of the most absurd experiences they've ever lived through has to be boot camp, and there are usually a few classic stories that follow. My version was Navy OCS – Officer Candidate School – and to a bit of a lesser extent, the police academy. I only say lesser not to demean the experience, but rather simply because we got to go home every night and we were on an eight-hour workday schedule. Add to that the fact that I had already been through my first boot camp experience, so the shock value wasn't there for me in the way it was to some of the newcomers.

Boot camps are breeding grounds for absurdity and the surreal. They're all a little different, but they're all essentially the same. You get yelled at, you exercise to exhaustion, you yell, you march, you get in line and shape up. It's all measured applications of stress, all designed to break you down to the lowest common denominator and form you into a moldable rookie version of whatever it is you're training to be.

The absurdity starts once you get into the real swing of things. Phil told me one about his time in the Marines. As an enlisted Marine, he was able to make it through most of the first several weeks of boot camp with a whole host of "Yes sir!", "No sir!", and "Aye aye sir!"'s. They got to one point when they were about four weeks in that his Drill Instructor addressed one of the recruits and asked him a question directly, demanding an answer beyond what the typical "Aye aye!" or "Yes sir!" or "No sir!" response would get him.

As the Drill Instructor repeatedly asked the question, getting more and more angry at the recruit for simply responding "Yes sir!" Phil finally chimed in.

"Sir, Private Heredia requesting permission to speak, sir!"

"What is it, Heredia!"

"Sir, Private Montes doesn't speak English, sir!"

The Drill Instructor, baffled, demands answers from Phil. "You shitting me or what, he doesn't speak goddamn English?"

"Sir, no sir, he speaks Spanish sir!"

"How did he get this far?"

"Sir, I don't know, sir!"

"Alright, then you translate for him!"

Heredia lowers his voice and speaks to Private Montes directly in a hushed tone. Montes, suddenly realizing what was being asked of him, gets this surprised, googly eyed look on his face, and answers back to Heredia, who relays the message back to the Drill Instructor.

"Heredia, you're his translator from now on. Now grab your goddamn rifles and get back in formation!"

Together the two of them, "Sir, aye aye, sir!"

It's hard to say what's more absurd about that story, the fact that Montes was recruited in the first place, the fact that he made it as far as he did not even speaking the language, or that he stayed in and somehow promoted faster than Phil. Or maybe the most surreal realization came from the Drill Instructor, suddenly realizing how ridiculous the situation was, and that after the hellish experience of having served two back-to-back combat tours, it all somehow culminated in him being the one who was somehow presiding over the absurdity.

*   *   *

Navy OCS starts on a Sunday. You arrive by car that morning and are directed to a parking lot. As you're getting out, someone in fatigues walks buy and instructs you to disconnect your car battery so it doesn't drain, because you won't have a chance to come start it for the next three and a half months. So you pop the hood, disconnect your battery, grab your duffel bag with your limited pairs of civilian clothes and the few items you were instructed to bring along, and make your way into the first building.

They bring you in groups of six and instruct you to stand at attention on yellow footprint markings on the ground. Then three Candi-O's – short for Candidate Officers – storm into the stairwell and march down the staircase. These are recruits who have made it to the final three weeks of training and have taken over command of the regiment, to simulate the experience of being in a leadership role, which is where everyone is ultimately headed following

OCS. All you hear are the synchronous slamming of boots against the floor, echoing down and into your body. You can't see anything, you have no idea what's coming, all you have is unease and nervous anticipation. It's the beginning of a feeling that will permeate your very soul and dominate your experience for the remainder of your time there, that sense of unease.

And then these three, sharp, uniformed soon to be Naval Officers appear as silhouettes against a backlit window one flight of stairs above you, so you're literally looking up to them, just amplifying how domineering their presence really is. Then the one in the middle gives a command to the other two, "Parade, rest!" They all shift their feet in unison, it's crisp. The one in the middle recites some inspiring get-tough type words and finishes it off with a dramatic "Welcome to OCS." Then all hell breaks loose.

What seems like an entire platoon of these guys storms in and begins yelling at you, barking the rules at you, and goddammit you're not loud enough, you're not sounding off loud enough, you need to be *ballistic* at all times, you tracking?

They introduce you to the basic rules of the place in the most overwhelming and loud way possible. They get way too close, kind of like how Chukums was with Sabrina, but they don't actually touch you because this isn't the 1970's anymore and they can't physically put their hands on you unless you give them permission first. So of course, when they need to physically correct you because your hands are not at your side properly and your feet are not where they are supposed to be at the proper position of attention or parade rest, the solution is to yell as loudly as they possibly can directly into your face, "Permission to touch?!" And because you're so caught up in the moment, there's no way you're going to *deny* them permission to touch you. So now they can grab you and physically correct you and ensure you are doing it fucking right. Because you gave them permission.

Everywhere you go, you are expected to *move with a purpose.* Everything you say you will say *ballistically,* which means scream at the top of your lungs. If you haven't lost your voice by the third day, you're not being ballistic enough. Your shoes are laced up wrong, untie them and lace them up the right way, outboard over inboard, which means the outside lace goes over the inside lace. And once you tie your shoes in a double not, tuck them into the side of your sneaker, because you're not a sloppy nasty civilian anymore, you need to look crisp at all times and can't have loose shoelaces flopping around like flaccid dicks on your feet.

Everything you say needs to be preceded by and followed up with a ballistic "Sir!" or "Ma'am!" You answer "Sir, yes sir!" or "Sir, no sir!" when asked a yes or no question. For everything else it is "Sir, aye aye sir!" to acknowledge you heard whatever it was that you were told. And don't fuck it up, that's a bad day for everybody.

The first three days are a whirlwind of absolute chaos, which is all just your company and your assigned crew of Candi-O's. They teach you the basics of how to exist at OCS so that when you are introduced to your Class Drill Instructor on Wake Up Wednesday you won't be completely lost.

Because if you think the Candi-O's are rough, just wait til you meet your Drill Instructor. Nobody's quit and rung the bell yet, but once the Drill Instructors are introduced, things get serious really fast.

The living quarters aren't what you would normally associate with the boot camp image of an open squad bay with twenty bunk beds, enough for a forty-man platoon.

The building layout for the regiment was a massive large hallway which was affectionately called the kill zone. The thinking is don't get caught in the kill zone, because everything there is fair game, no matter which company you were in or which Drill Instructor you were assigned to. Anyone could jack you up if you got caught in the kill zone.

Extending out of the kill zone like centipedes were perpendicular branches. Each branch was a passageway, or p-way, with individual two person rooms, like how a college dorm might be set up. Each p-way hosted one company. Two people per hatch, ten hatches on one side, and ten hatches directly across on the other side. The p-way was big enough where two people could face directly across from each other in a slightly staggered formation while in the pushup position – a position we would frequently find ourselves in.

The Candi-O's introduce you to chow hall procedures, which is a serious fucking evolution – it's a way of marching into the chow hall, receiving your food, sitting at your table, and eating your meal. There's a checklist for everything, and getting chow is no different.

Navy OCS is the only boot camp where chow hall is a strictly regimented affair. Normally when you think of chow hall at a boot camp, you envision a bunch of bald-headed recruits stuffing as much food as they possibly can down their gullets over the course of maybe thirty seconds to a minute, just to get the calories in as fast as humanly possible because there's more training to be done and you aren't there to relax and have a meal. In Navy OCS, every chow meal is a forty-five-minute evolution. It usually takes about fifteen minutes to march to just outside the chow hall in formation, the class leader announces the order, "Company, prepare for chow hall procedures!"

"Prepare for chow hall procedures, aye aye sir!"

And the guidon posts the guidon to let everyone know which class is in the chow hall, so if they are slacking or randomly happen to piss someone off or otherwise fuck up, everybody knows which class did it, and there will be hell to pay later. Then everyone marches in step one column at a time, perfectly to the cadence.

Once everyone marches through and is served their trays of food, they grab a spoon and a glass of water and a glass of Gatorade and make their way to the table and place the tray down. They remain standing and pull out a pocket-sized regulation manual and open it up and hold out their arm parallel to the deck and study, arm fully outstretched.

Hopefully you are one of the last people to come through the line, because after holding your arm out for more than a couple minutes, a small booklet of paper somehow manages to become unbearably heavy.

Once everyone is at the table, the order is given to be seated. Everyone sits at the position of attention, and whoever is heading the chow hall operation gives the orders, be it your Candi-O or your Drill Instructor. This is called eating by the numbers, and they count off each step.

"One!" Everyone snaps their heads down and looks at the plate of food.

"Two!" With your left hand, grab the spoon which is arranged to the right of your plate, and hold it at a ready position to engage the food on the plate below.

"Three!" In one motion, scoop up a bite of food and hold it at the ready.

"Four!" Deposit the food in your mouth.

"Five!" Remove the spoon and place it back on the right side of your plate.

"Six!" Snap your head back up.

"Seven!" Chew and swallow your food.

"Eight!" Using your left hand, extend it out and grab a glass of your preferred beverage, either the water or Gatorade and raise it so your extended arm is parallel to the deck.

"Nine!" Take one drink.

"Ten!" Put the glass back and return to the position of seated attention.

This process repeats over and over again for about twenty minutes. Thing is, it takes so long to get one bite of food, that twenty minutes isn't nearly enough time to get any actual food into your system, so you are operating on a major calorie deficit the entire time. Not to mention, it isn't exactly easy to eat a slice of roast beef with a spoon, and it's even harder to get a scoop large enough onto said spoon in one piercing motion. The result is a bunch of starving, despondent bald-headed guys and girls with no makeup all staring awkwardly across from each other with hunks of roast beef hanging out their mouths, maintaining thousand-yard stares, refusing to break their military bearing, because to do so would mean death in the kill zone.

Chow was such a serious matter that on one particular occasion, a guy named Lewisberry, while eating a bite of creamed spinach, suddenly got the urge to sneeze. He held it as long as he could, but in the end, a torrent of green spewed from his face directly at this guy Eric sitting directly across from him.

Eric didn't fucking move.

Not even a flinch as spinach bits painted his face, not unlike Marvin's brains in Pulp Fiction. Eric was a fucking champ and Lewisberry shined his boots for him the next three nights. We started calling him Green Mist.

Once you get accustomed to the routine of it all, it becomes manageable enough. You come to expect random explosive exercise sessions, known as RPT – Remedial Physical Training – remedial, because to just randomly punish you with exercise would be considered hazing unless it was serving some greater purpose, namely that you're a fat nasty thing and need to shed some pounds.

Some people are just naturally good at boot camp, others struggle with the whole military discipline part of it. Personally, I adjusted fairly well, which isn't to say I didn't have my fuckups for which the whole company suffered the consequences. I distinctly remember forgetting to brace the bulkhead (read "wall") when addressing a Drill Instructor, which promptly earned everyone in my general vicinity a solid five minutes of pushups and squats.

Another guy named Colin earned us all a really rough session during drill practice. Drill practice is when we all form up with our inert M16 rifles and go through ceremonial drill movements – left shoulder, right shoulder, port arms, order arms, inspection arms. Colin forgot how to go from port arms to order arms and was the only one standing with his rifle still in front of his chest while everyone else was standing with the rifles at their sides.

Believing it was just a brain fart, our Drill Instructor calls out for him to correct himself. Instead of performing the movement, Colin screams "Sir, aye aye sir!"

And then he just stands there.

Drill Instructor comes over to him and yells at him to correct himself. Another "Sir, aye aye sir!" And then nothing. Finally, the Drill Instructor yells at him, "Don't tell me fucking aye aye and then don't do what I'm telling you to do, you dirtbag!" He snatches the rifle from him, chucks it a mile across the gym, and barks out at our whole company, "Get on your faces! All of you! Start pushing!" We all each lost about five pounds of sweat that afternoon in an RPT session that lasted maybe forty-five minutes – forty-five minutes of pure, constant exercise. It just wouldn't end. From that day forward, Colin's nickname was Dirtbag.

It wasn't all just explosive chaos. The unpredictability of it all sometimes drove the punishment. Our Drill Instructor was known for his mind games. We never knew when we were getting the ballistic crazy coked up Marine Corps Drill Instructor or the sadistic psychopath who smiled in subtle enjoyment as he watched us suffer in anticipation of a punishment that may or may not come.

Take Rosati, my hatch mate, who fell asleep while standing at attention while our Drill Instructor was giving us a lecture. He didn't punish all of us. Instead, he asked, almost feigning concern, "Rosati, are you tired? You been getting enough sleep?"

"Sir, I haven't slept much lately, sir."

"Ok. Pick a friend."

Rosati panics and points out the first person he notices making eye contact with him. "Officer Candidate Yu!"

"Yu, both you and Rosati start pushing."

Together in unison, Yu and Rosati, "Sir, aye aye sir!" And gunny kept right on giving his lecture right where he left off, didn't miss a beat. Eventually he finished speaking and there were two giant sweat puddles on the ground beneath two huffing bald guys in fatigues. That's OCS for you. You never know how you're gonna get roped in.

*   *   *

You come to develop a strange mindset, being immersed in such bizarre conditions. It's like how prisoners don't remember how to do normal life once they get out of jail because they've become so institutionalized. OCS was strange in a similar way. You start to develop little cheat codes to make it work for you.

Because nobody could ever get enough calories in during chow hall, a black market of snacks and food developed after lights out. Some guys had the hookup from classes more senior to us because they got rolled back into our company due to injuries or failures. The senior recruits, who had less watchful eyes on them, were able to sneak out goodies from the chow hall and passed them to their buddies late at night, and people would barter for them. Picture a beefed-up recruit, a former powerlifter, desperate for calories sneaking around like a goddamn ninja up to an unmarked door. Three light knocks and the door cracks open, not unlike at a crack house.

"I heard you got peanut butter in here, let me get some of that, I need the protein."

In the moment it all makes sense, but take a step back and it's way more absurd than you realized.

Unlike prison, showers were somehow always the most relaxing part of the day, simply because at the end of the day there's nobody there to fuck with you, and you get a moment to let your guard down and feel refreshed after a day that likely included a ton of exercise sweating in the sand pits outside. And after being locked on all damn day with impeccable military bearing, finally a moment where you can tell jokes and talk shit without worrying about a Drill Instructor bursting in is a welcome relief.

Make no mistake, somebody would always end up singing and a handful of other people would jump in and start belting out verses to classic rock hits. A welcome moment of peace, until it's all ruined when somebody gets a little too comfortable and starts pissing in the shower, running stinky pee all over everyone's feet.

Suddenly that carefree song turns into a chorus of angry, "Who's the motherfucker pissing like a little bitch, I'll fucking destroy you, you fucking bitch-ass motherfucking child!" Nobody ever admitted they were the one who took a piss in the communal shower, but we all suspect it was probably Lewisberry.

Years later when reflecting on the bizarre nature of OCS, with all its absurdity and the surreal experience of living it, it astounds me that my experiences were not entirely unique. Thousands upon thousands of Sailors and Marines and Soldiers and Airmen all went through similar experiences, and in that shared experience there is perhaps some universal truth that can be inferred. Maybe it's as simple as sweating and bleeding and showering with someone that will form a human bond that can only be understood by someone who has lived through it themselves. I still throw that one out at my wife whenever she thinks me and my OCS buddies are getting a little carried away in our antics, usually while drinking. "Honey, we've showered together, you wouldn't get it!"

"Why do you guys always say that?! It's so weird!"

"It is what it is babe."

OCS wasn't just bizarre for the recruits going through it. Take Sam's caper, a skinny white kid with glasses from Missouri. We're sitting in our p-way one afternoon with about two hours of free time til our next evolution, so the time is being spent prepping for an upcoming inspection. People are in their hatches staging clothes, ironing uniforms, sitting in the hallway and shooting the shit while shining their boots. Sam gets the urge to take a piss. He drops his shoes and walks down the p-way towards the main kill zone and takes a peek through the glass to make sure the coast is clear. Sure enough, there is another company out there getting absolutely smoked by their Drill Instructor. Sam wants no part of that, so he decides to wait a few minutes until they finish.

Two minutes go by. Then Four. Then ten. Then fifteen. Poor Sam's bladder is about to burst.

One thing I never mentioned, is that you are encouraged to constantly hydrate because you never know when your next PT session will come. The constant hydration means everyone is constantly pissing. Sam, unable to hold it, and not wanting to venture into the kill zone, retreats back into his hatch and finds a one-gallon Ziplock bag and relieves himself. He finishes, zips it up, and secures it in his wall locker in his hatch.

The day goes by like normal, and towards the end of the day we're all back in our hatches with a little time before lights out. Sam remembers the bag of piss and decides now is a good time to go and trash it in the bathroom. He grabs his Ziplock bag full of clear yellowish liquid and makes his way to the main door into the kill zone. He peers through the glass, checks left, checks right, coast is clear. He pops open the door and ventures out.

No sooner than he's twenty paces from the bathroom that another Drill Instructor rounds the corner and is coming straight at him. These guys are supposed to be gone for the night! But Sam is not one to get rattled. He stops dead in his tracks, braces the bulkhead, assumes the position of attention, and belts out the greeting of the day, "Attention on deck, standby! Good evening, sir!"

The Drill Instructor has no idea who this kid is, but it's not the first time one of these guys has stopped dead in the hallway at the mere sight of him, they were well trained. But this kid is carrying something. Looks a bit odd.

"What you got there, candidate?"

Sam maintains his thousand-yard stare and pauses for a moment. The Drill Instructor can sense he's searching for a sensible answer.

"It's a bag of urine, sir!"

Quizzically, "Alright, carry on."

"Sir, aye aye, sir!" Sam resumes his beeline for the bathroom, thankful that was the end of that exchange. The drill instructor continues on his way, shaking his head and not knowing what to make of it.

Kind of like being on hour nine of a ten-hour shift and suddenly seeing a giant white van coming around a corner with a fat black lady about to shit herself and an almost naked Asian guy named Jimmy in the passenger seat screaming he's being kidnapped. Sometimes there's just nothing left to say. Absurd and surreal.

Ensign Larry

Despite what they may tell you, you *can* in fact have your cake and eat it too.

I first met Ensign Larry when he was still an Officer Candidate at Naval Station Newport, Rhode Island. Our first interaction wasn't much of an interaction at all, but more of a first impression, lasting image of the guy.

Larry was a class ahead of me and I happened to be passing through their p-way one evening. His class was preparing for an inspection, and mostly everyone was sitting on the floor while shining their dress shoes, while others were inside their hatches ironing their khaki uniforms.

Everyone was clustered around in small little groups of three or four people, mostly based on where their rooms were. I first noticed Larry sitting towards the end of the p-way, intently trying to get a brilliant shine on his shoes. He was sitting alone. As I walked in that direction, I casually asked him if he had seen his class leader, that I had a question for him. He responded in kind. I accomplished what I needed to, the night went on.

I didn't see Larry again until I got down to Pensacola, Florida after OCS. It was around April of 2011. Once I arrived, I met up with a few of the guys from OCS who were also in the flight school pipeline and we got to talking. Enter Josh, the other key player in this story.

Josh is from Columbus, Ohio, but if it weren't for his mid-west Ohio boy accent, you would peg him as being somewhere from the east coast, maybe south Jersey or Philly. He's always had a sense of style and swagger that you wouldn't normally associate with the mid-west.

Me coming from New York, he looked like any of the guidos you would run into on the bar scene, dressed up, classy shirt, trim pants, hair styled, with a drink in one hand and a girl on the other arm. Maybe two. Probably two.

Once we got to Pensacola, it was much more Alabama than Miami. Neither of us really knew anybody down there aside from the few people we went to OCS with, and the going out scene was a bit of a culture shock. Lotta plaid shirts and ballcaps, everyone very much dressed down – definitely not your New York nightlife scene. That's why we initially hit it off, as Josh's expectation of "going out" was much more in line with mine – when you go out, you dress accordingly. You don't go out looking like you just got done tilling a farm.

My wife Nikki, originally from San Diego and who I met in college in New York, was already institutionalized by the big city. She was now a product of Washington Heights and the Bronx just from being with me and living there for six years. She was also thrown headfirst into life in the deep south, accompanying me on the beginnings of a military career.

The three of us formed a pretty tight knit trio. Turns out, she was the best wingman for Josh and our single friends. She was married, out with her husband, and with the both of us essentially winging for the rest of the crew, it couldn't have gotten any easier for these guys.

We started hanging out with Larry, who was also in Pensacola for flight school and ended up rooming with Josh. It became kind of a regular thing, the four of us getting together, going out for drinks, Sunday dinners, hanging out at the house, road trips to New Orleans.

Larry had never been the "going out" type. Prior to joining the military, he spent most of his time hanging out in his room on the computer, rarely leaving except for bathroom breaks. He was shy and overweight.

Josh told me Larry admitted to him he once didn't leave his room for nine weeks straight. His mom would just bring him food while he played video games and wrote code.

Eventually he got sick of that life, lost some weight, finished college, and joined the Navy. Fast forward four months, welcome to Pensacola.

When he got to Florida, Larry came clean to all of us, said he wanted to make a change. Sure, he was a Naval Officer and attending flight school, and making decent money for a young Ensign in his mid-twenties. But he wasn't a social guy, had zero sense of style, and hadn't really been with any women save for maybe once or twice over the years.

He wanted to be the social butterfly type of person who could walk into a bar, strike up a conversation with the bartender and a couple of random women, and before you know it be taking shots with everyone. That's what he wanted. He wanted the feeling of having a good-looking girl on his arm like I had, and the confidence and style of Josh to make it all become a reality.

I have to say, bravo to the guy. It takes real balls to come out and admit you are unhappy with yourself and commit to making a change. We all respected it, and still do. Josh agreed to take him under his wing.

First step was to get Larry a new wardrobe. All he was wearing were old sports team t-shirts.

Enough.

He tossed all of those and picked out some fitted jeans, some nice shirts, a vest, a few accessories like a bracelet, a necklace, a new jacket, and to top it all off, a fedora. Larry really leaned into the whole fedora thing. It was a bit off-putting, but who were we to step on this guy's newfound sense of style? And realistically, if he could nail the other social efforts, the fedoras could serve as a conversation piece at the very least. Harmless overall.

Second was to get him into some bars. It was a team effort. After a few times out with the three of us, Larry became a natural at the social interactions. Before long, we would find ourselves starting out with our little group which would soon blossom into a group of seven or eight by the end of the night. Nikki and I would peel away to go do our thing, and the rest would splinter off and have a night of their own.

Here's where it started to go sideways. Josh was a prior enlisted sailor and had traveled the world. He had made port at several different locations on cruise, and at one point lived in Thailand for almost a year. As you would expect from a dirty ass sailor, he had experienced all kinds of wild sex and alcohol and drug fueled escapades over the years.

Josh would tell us all these stories, and Josh, as you can imagine, is a master storyteller. Larry was hooked. I mean, he was enamored with all the filth and booze and chaos. This was what it was all about, and he was determined to live that life. He hit up Josh one afternoon and said, "Let's do it."

"Do what?"

"Go to Thailand, I want to go."

He was determined. Josh agreed, they put in their leave requests, booked two round trip tickets, and suddenly they were off to Bangkok.

About a week and a half goes by. Nikki and I are running errands when my phone starts buzzing.

"Hello?"

"Hey it's Josh, what's up man."

"We're good, how was the trip?"

"Man...I can't even get into it over the phone. You guys at your place?"

"No, we're finishing up some shopping, heading back now. Where's Larry?"

"Bro...he is *on his way home*. I need to get away from him for a minute."

There's something in his voice that tells me something is wrong with Larry. "He ok?"

"I don't know, man. It got pretty fucking crazy. I'll meet you at your place, how does Dunkin sound?"

"Uhh ok, grab us two medium French vanillas, maybe a couple donuts?"

"Sounds good, be there in thirty."

Nikki says to me after I hang up, "Did you and Josh just make plans for tonight?"

"Yeah, he's bringing donuts and coffee. Something about the trip being crazy, I have no idea."

Fast forward about forty-five minutes and we're all sitting in my living room. The coffee is hot, the fragrant aroma of French vanilla wafting through the air. It's four in the afternoon but it smells like breakfast.

Josh is sitting in the chair across from Nikki and me. We settle back into the couch with our coffees. Josh pulls out a laptop from his backpack and starts fumbling with the power cord. "I've got evidence, before I say anything."

"What do you mean, evidence?"

"There's video, bro. Video, and photos, it's insanity."

"Where is Larry, he make it back?"

"Yeah, he's home now, but I just had to get away because I need to get this off my chest."

We nod along accordingly.

"So remember how before we left he kept making a point of telling me not to let him get involved with a ladyboy, right?"

Remember, this is 2011. This is back before they added the "T" to the LGBT acronym. It was there, but nobody really knew anything about it. It was an anomaly, more shocking than anything, an oddity. The most exposure anybody had to anything trans related we got from The Hangover Part Two, and coincidentally, from stories people would bring back from places overseas like Thailand or the Philippines.

"Yeah, we remember."

"And I promised, wholeheartedly, that I wouldn't let him get drunk and take one home, I'm not that big of an asshole."

"No, you're a good guy."

"I mean, I love my mom, pay my taxes, I'm not gonna let my friend get involved with a ladyboy if he makes me promise to keep an eye on him."

"Naturally, we wouldn't let you in our house if you were *that* much of an asshole," I reply. We're on board.

Josh starts into it. The first night, they touch down in Bangkok around 10pm local time. It was Larry's first flight overseas so he was tired, but also excited to see what the streets of Bangkok held in store for him.

Josh gives him a rundown of how things work since this is all literally foreign. Bar fines, ST vs LT, pick pockets, ladyboys, drink prices, some basic Thai phrases, taxis, overall safety items, the whole nine.

I interrupt Josh to slow him down, "Bar fines? What is it you're telling him?"

Josh explains to us that at the bars, there are going to be tons of girls who specifically work for the bar. When you're in the bar, they essentially hook you in and get you to buy more and more drinks. Eventually you're going to want to leave with the girl, but guess what – now you're taking her away from the bar, and the bar is going to be losing money because the girl won't be there to work customers. So you pay the girl for whatever you're going to do with her, but you also pay a fine directly to the bar. Hence, a bar fine.

They leave their hotel on Soi 19 and head towards Soi Cowboy. By now it's around 12:30am and they've already got a little buzz going from the drinks they lifted from the mini bar.

Near Soi Cowboy, a group of girls yells at them from their taxi which is stopped at a red light. Ready for

119

adventure, they run over to the taxi, dodging and weaving around the mess of cars, and hop in the taxi with the girls. Good start.

Larry sits in the front seat on one of the girls' laps and Josh jumps in the backseat and lays across all three. They're heading wherever the girls are, and it looks like it's to a bar called Insomnia Bangkok. They arrive at Insomnia and enter through the restaurant below.

First up is about nine shots of Sambuca. If you've never had Sambuca, it's an Italian liquor which has a strong taste of black licorice, best served ice cold. It's a unique kind of shot. The first time you take it, it hits hard. Makes you feel like your stomach is on fire, and if you throw it up, your esophagus feels like a melting candy cane. It gets easier with each subsequent night out.

Nine shots, and Larry thinks they are for all of them. Negative. He's out with Josh in Thailand, no way they're starting out weak – five for Josh, four for Larry.

Larry's not a drinker, never has been. But they hit the ground running. He forces down all four shots like a champ, they walk upstairs, order a round of beers, and start their prowl around the club.

It's worth mentioning here that the initial group of girls they came in with weren't the most attractive bunch, but who's keeping track? A typical Thai nightclub scene plays out, and after some more beers, a few syringe shots, several girls grabbing hold of Larry's junk, and another round of Sambuca, Larry wasn't looking so good. Sweat beading on his brow, eyes glazed over, that licorice candy cane smell starting to ferment in his gut.

He had been out with us in Pensacola, he had even done Sambuca shots with Josh and me, but he had never drunk this much. Hell, he'd never been this drunk and had a handful of random girls grab his dick in a club either, for that matter. It's a night of firsts.

As they make their way back through the smoky, loud, noisy bar, they pass the initial group of girls who had settled down in a corner and were sharing a hookah pipe. They stop for a quick picture. Josh shows us the picture. Larry looks disheveled, to put it lightly. That fedora is sitting crooked on his head, you can tell nothing positive was happening at this point – it's definitely an end of the night photo. They head back to the hotel, Josh drops Larry off at his room, then heads back out. Party on.

The next morning Josh wakes up around 2pm and finds a small handwritten note under his door. It reads, "Josh, went for food. I will be ok. Love, Larry."

Josh panics. What time did he leave? How long has he been out? This guy doesn't speak a lick of Thai and has never been outside the states, and now he's searching Bangkok for food.

He rushes over to Larry's room, knocks, holds his breath. A shuffling noise. Thank God, he's there. He opens the door, the panic subsides.

They gather their things and venture out into town, causally debriefing the previous evening. Larry confirms he's never been that drunk before, has never experienced such a wild time. Josh tells him to stand by, because that was just the first night, the trip is going to be more than memorable.

Larry tells Josh about a problem he has, seemingly out of nowhere. He starts out that he's really inexperienced with women, and that for most of his years he's been pleasuring himself with his hands, so when he finally hooked up with a woman he couldn't finish because it didn't feel the same. It took him forever to finally come. Josh is thinking, ok forever, sure. So what, it took him twenty, maybe thirty minutes? Little did he know...

Before long they find themselves standing in front a building advertising massages. They could both use one to recuperate. And a real massage, not a happy ending massage. This place appears to be official, so the lack of seediness lends to the idea it will be a normal experience.

They walk inside, and it opens up into a nicely lit foyer. They're greeted by an attractive girl in her early twenties, she grabs each of them by the hand and begins leading them upstairs. Surely enough, Josh begins to realize they will in fact be offered a happy ending. Oh well, not the worst thing that could happen.

Each of them is led into a separate room. It takes about forty-five minutes before it all erupts into chaos. While Josh is enjoying himself, Larry finds himself laying down on the massage table, stripped down and comfortable.

Almost immediately, the girl goes down on him. And she starts working him. She's a pro. Larry has never felt anything even remotely like this back home in his limited experience. And she's working him and working him and sucking and gagging and cupping the balls and working the shaft and *nothing*.

She goes hard for about thirty minutes, likely with each passing minute questioning her womanhood. At this point it's a challenge, why won't he come?

She decides to up her massage game. She gets on top and begins riding him. This motherfucker is gonna make her work for it. Alright, bring it white boy. She starts riding, and she starts going faster, and faster, and faster, and then...*nothing*.

"Why you no come?!" she demands in her broken English. "Why, I go hard, you no come! What wrong?"

Larry replies, "No, I'm sorry it's ok, it's not you, it's no problem, I'm going to wait for my friend."

Except he doesn't just say it in a regular accent, he says it in a weird, pseudo-Thai accent that really just sounds pandering and for some reason Jamaican. Imagine Larry trying to explain to this poor woman who just put in forty-five minutes of hard work with no results, to the point it's an actual insult to her womanhood, and he does it in a weird Jamaican Rastafarian sounding accent. Like Bob Marley nervously explaining that he *doesn't* want a blowjob.

"Oh, you want friend? I bring you my friend, you have two lady!"

Larry rebuffs, "No no, no other lady, I wait for *my* friend, *my* friend."

Immediately she gets upset with him, "You bad man! No two man one lady, not good, you bad man!"

She storms into the hallway causing a ruckus, this is bullshit, she's out there doing a job, sucking dick and riding this Jamaican sounding motherfucker and he wants to gangbang her, no way, that's not what she signed up for, these sick Americans –

123

Mamasan rushes up the stairs ready to back up her girl. This isn't the first time one of the clients has gotten out of line. Josh rushes out in his robe and starts playing referee. Larry is standing there confused, speechless, not even understanding what the hell just happened. Chalk it up to cultural differences. The argument spirals, they drop some cash, grab their things, and take off. Another strikeout for Larry.

Later that night, Larry again gets too drunk to bring anyone home. Maybe next time.

Third night in Bangkok Josh decides to take Larry out for his first gogo experience at Babydolls. It's not long before he has a sexy thing sitting on his lap, hands down his pants and her tongue down his throat. He's in heaven, better than the massage place.

He's got a few drinks in him, it's less awkward, more of a social setting as opposed to a place where he can just be uncomfortable and awkward with one other person. Now it's all about the social cues, which remember from his training in Pensacola, he's gotten much better at.

This goes on for a bit before they decide to leave. Josh makes him leave without his girl, doesn't want to bar fine him on his first gogo, after all. They make it to three other gogos before he turns to Josh and gives him a look, and declares without reservation, "I'm going back for Lek."

He couldn't stop him, and why would he? Have at it, that's why you're here, have yourself an adventure, Larry.

They meet back up, Larry with his newfound girl on his arm (short a bit of cash), and the trio parties on for a couple more hours until Josh finds some action, then they split ways for the night.

The next morning, Josh wakes up at 11am and calls Larry. It rings. It keeps ringing. He knows he made it back to the hotel, why isn't he picking up? Rings a few more times, and then it finally answers. No hello, no greeting. Just an awful panting into the phone. And then a groan under someone's breath.

"Larry? What the hell man, you there?"

"Hey Josh."

"Are you...still fucking? It's 11am!"

"Is it?" Larry sounds honestly dumbstruck.

"Have you been fucking for the last eight hours or something?" Josh says jokingly with a laugh.

"Has it been that long?"

Josh's tone shifts. "Yeah dude, it's 11am, we got back at three." Eight hours, that's a full workday.

"Oh wow, time got away from me."

"I'm heading downstairs, come get some breakfast."

"Ok I'll meet you down there in an hour."

He hangs up. No way this man has been fucking for the last eight hours, that's insane. Pornstars don't fuck for that long. Prostitutes don't fuck for that long. Nobody does, that'd be insane. Nothing lasts that long except of course, for full workdays.

An hour later Larry comes sauntering into the dining room with his girl on his arm, and they both look beat. Worn the hell out. They look like they've both been through battle.

The poor girl couldn't walk straight. Josh gets this horrified look on his face, both of shock and surprise, absolutely appalled. Who does this? Who fucks like this?

They sit down and he chats up the girl, and she confirms it. He fucked her for over eight hours, and *finally* he came. Just once. One pop, that's it. Not only did he come, but he blasted inside her once she got fed up and ripped the condom off. Consequences be damned, she finally finished the marathon and got the fucking of her life.

The next night Larry met his match: Cake.

They started nearly every night at Cherry Bar. One of Josh's old friends from back when he lived in Thailand runs the place, so it's a good place to get started. Fun, honest company, lively environment, good energy, cheap drinks.

One caveat: all the girls in Cherry Bar are ladyboys.

Now here's a point of distinction, it's not considered culturally taboo in Thailand and other parts of southeast Asia, not the way it is in the states. And the term "ladyboy" when referring to trans individuals, is a very distinct class in and of itself. While a trans person technically is someone who is undergoing or has already transitioned, and a ladyboy technically fits that bill, all trans men to women are not ladyboys, even though all ladyboys are technically trans. Ladyboys inhabit the entertainment space, embodying the natural sex appeal of the effeminate, with the mystique of still being something a bit more adventurous and off the beaten path. Two sides of the same coin, cousins in concept.

Remember, in 2011 the simple concept of gay marriage wasn't even widely tolerated as an acceptable thing. Consider in the 2008 presidential race, when then candidate Barack Obama famously said he believed marriage was between a man and a woman, and it wasn't until the 2012 re-election that he shifted on the issue. Politically driven decisions, sure, but politics so often shape public perception, or more accurately, are a reflection of that public perception.

Ten years later, gay marriage, trans acceptance, it's a different story. Bangkok is just the epicenter of it, a place built on the exploitation of man's desire for sexual adventure and self-discovery. It's just a part of the cultural landscape that there are entire bars which feature ladyboys, and Cherry Bar is one of them.

That first night at Cherry Bar, Cake immediately takes a liking to Larry. Cake is in fact a ladyboy, but easily mistaken as a woman. As they get to flirting, Josh whispers to Larry off to the side, "You know Cake is a ladyboy, right?"

"You sure?"

"Yes, Cake is a ladyboy."

The flirting continued. She'd touch him subtly, rub against him, giggle when he'd make a pass at her, playing it up in the back and forth. Larry knew Cake was a ladyboy, but he couldn't hide the fact that a part of him really liked it, the attention and the naughtiness of it. Josh grabbed him and off they went.

The second night at Cherry Bar, Larry tells Josh "You know it's Cake's birthday today."

He wanted to stop at 7-11 and buy her a cake, "Because her name is Cake." Obviously.

He stops and buys her a cake, and then back to the bar. He surprises her with the cake, and at that point, she knows she has him. She's in his head if he remembered her birthday, gonna be putty in her hands. She continues flirting with him, except much heavier this time – grabbing his junk, rubbing him, making him grab her tits, the full monty.

Josh grabs him and they leave. The third night at Cherry Bar, it finally goes down. She's all over him. Josh is talking to his friend at the bar, and when he turns his head back towards Larry, low and behold, they're making out hardcore. It's less two people making out and more two people battling each other with their tongues. Josh rushes over to him and saves him for a third time.

Nikki and I are on the edge of our seats, both repulsed and intrigued. It's truly a car crash you can't look away from, and we know where this story is going. We fear where this story is going. Nobody sets up a story about an introvert's sexual awakening by describing an eight-hour sex marathon for nothing. It's the precursor to me turning around to find a man in a holding tank, bouncing up and down, looking determined as ever while the rhythm plays out…whooaa, tainted love.

I fear that by the end of this story, there is going to be a thumb up an ass.

Josh pulls open a video window on his computer and hits play. No shit, there is Cake manhandling Larry, the both of them making out hard in a club, and out pops a titty.

To say it is grotesque is an understatement. They're like two snakes trying to swallow each other's heads.

It's aggressive, about what you'd expect two sloppy drunks embracing passionately in a club to look like, grabbing each other in uncontrolled ecstasy. Except something is slightly off because although the woman *appears* to be a woman, there's something subtle about her body and the way she moves that makes her seem like a man. And worse than any of that, Cake is wearing Larry's fedora. It's gone full circle and then some.

Josh closes the video, "I told you guys this got crazy."

They're on the baht bus and Larry says to Josh, "If I don't find a lady by 1am I'm going back for Cake."

They make it to *one* gogo and then Larry turns to him, giving that look of serious intensity, a man determined. It was 10:30pm.

"You're sure you want to do this? You need to be sure."

"I'm good. I'll meet you back at the bar."

Like clockwork, in walks Larry with Cake on his arm. He couldn't believe it, he actually went back for her. Josh was buzzed, but this sobered him right up.

They're in FLB for no more than five minutes when they get extreme with the makeouts, worse than before. Cake is slamming him up against the wall, violently manhandling him, and he's loving it. At one point, their teeth literally bang together, clackety clack.

They continue, letting the evening take them where it may. Out pops another titty, and Larry beelines for it, sucking like he's stranded in the Mojave and whatever is in there is gonna save him. Is it water? Is it milk? Does Cake's titty even make milk?

Here's our friend, adamant in the weeks leading up to the trip, that he doesn't want to hook up with a ladyboy, now publicly swapping spit and sucking on her tits. It's too much for Josh. He bids them goodnight and takes off. They'll catch up in the morning.

Around noon the next day, Larry stumbles down to breakfast. He's got a limp which alternates between each leg and after each step, a slight wince. The man's spirit is broken, and from what it appears, half his body is too.

He looks like a Thai gang got hold of him in a back alley and spent the better part of the evening beating the hell out of him. But no gang – it was just Cake.

This is what ten rounds with Cake gets you. He has a hickey on his neck that looks like something only a horse's mouth could leave, and he has smaller ones all over his neck and body. He has a bruise about the size of a baseball on his thigh. Dried blood smears his shins, running down from both knees which have been rubbed raw. It even looks like some of his hair has been completely ripped out, and the man has short hair to begin with.

They venture up to his room and from the hallway, they're approaching with a sense of dread. I've been on that call before, the welfare check on someone nobody's been able to reach for a week. Usually it's an old person, sometimes a recovering addict. You're walking up there hoping in the back of your mind that maybe the guy is just on a good bender, or pissed at the jerkoff relative who doesn't have the balls to go track him down in person and instead sends the cops to do it. But in the back of your mind, you know. You don't want to admit it, but you know. Especially when you make your way up the stairwell and suddenly a breeze comes through, and you're struck with the smell. It's rancid, reeks of feces and rotting flesh. It's gonna be a stinker, might as well call the coroner now.

Josh and Larry open the door, and the smell hits them. It's similar, but the rotting flesh smell is replaced with a combination of alcohol, sex, lube, perfume, and Listerine. The feces smell is still present, and most definitely unmistakable. The floor is littered with empty water bottles. Blood and shit covered bed sheets are clustered in a pile on the floor at the foot of the bed, which sits at an uneven angle because one of the legs has been damaged, so the bed's limp matches Larry's.

"What the fuck happened here? Why are your knees all bloody?"

Larry points to the marble slab that makes up the base of the bed. Sure enough, blood stains on the mattress. "They were banging up against the side of the bed, we just got really into it."

One of the nightstands was broken to pieces, completely on its side. Same with the coffee table. Larry says they literally fucked all over the room. He even describes at one point he had a foot in the bathroom sink while he plowed Cake from behind.

There's a brown gelatinous substance on a tube of toothpaste, and an unspooled cannister of dental floss, also covered in the brown jelly.

Josh asks the question, knowing full well he doesn't want to know the answer.

"What is that?"

"It's shit. And lube. Got rough up on the sink."

Josh just looks at him, horrified. His eyes wide, he runs his hand through his hair, simply trying to process the scene.

"Don't worry, it's from Cake, not me."

As if that makes it better. As if now it makes sense, that it's Cake's and not his shit in the dental floss.

Then it dawns on Josh – wait, this was a ladyboy. No vagina? This was all…from behind? He asks Larry how it worked. Larry just waives it off, casually explaining it was no different than being with a woman. He went down on her, gave her oral and then banged her in her vagina that wasn't exactly a vagina but was pretty close and then they did anal, nothing odd about that. He ate his Cake. And it only took him three hours to finish this time, so that's progress.

Josh poses the question, "Wait, Cake was post-op, right? So how was it, was there any kind of...leftovers or anything? Or was it like a regular vagina, just normal?"

"It was normal, I didn't notice anything different on my end."

"Are you sure?" asks Josh, "What about the rest, like I get the tits were probably fake, and the vagina was probably pretty close, but what about the hands? And the bone structure and body frame and all the rest, was it like being with a guy at all? There's gotta be a difference, between being with an actual born woman versus a man, there are differences –

"No way, what are you talking about, it's nothing like that." Except he's not too sure.

Larry is way too worn out from his evening with Cake, so he decides to take a night off. Fast forward to the next evening, Larry has to give Josh a raincheck because he's spending the evening with Cake. He takes her to Beef Eater Steakhouse on Soi Diana Inn, one of the more high-end spots in town. After what they did to each other the other night, I suppose it was only the gentlemanly thing to do.

There's Larry, the man who so adamantly begged, who demanded, to be protected from getting involved with a ladyboy, out on a date, one of the stages of courtship, with Cake.

Over the course of the next several nights, sprinkled in with other instances of debauchery, he never forgot his

Cake. They talked every day and made plans for his final night in Bangkok.

By the time they got back to the room on that last night, the taxi was already scheduled to pick them up in less than three hours to take them to the airport. They had to work fast.

Josh listened nervously from the neighboring room. The banging and crashing sounds coming from the room were unreal. It did not sound like sex was happening in that room – it sounded like construction.

A couple hours later, the taxi arrived and Larry and Cake came walking out through the lobby. Cake was smiling ear to ear, absolutely glowing, like she had won some kind of championship bout. Larry looked defeated. Smelled like it too. Stale and expired, pale, dehydrated. A Marine Corps drill instructor couldn't have worked him over like this. His sweatpants were ripped down the seam, aside a massive ripped hole on one of the knees. It was just enough to distract from his bloodshot eyes and overall sense that his soul had been ripped from his body. You had to look a little closer to see that.

As they're getting ready to leave, Larry hugs Cake and tries to step into the taxi, letting out a slight groan as he hoists his bodyweight into the seat. Cake giggles and snaps his seatbelt for him, almost like a mother strapping in a small child. And just like a child, Larry is out within two minutes.

Several moments later, "I have a hickey on my scalp."

He shows Josh, and go figure, a sucker bite on top of his skull. Josh has never heard of anyone getting a hickey on their scalp, yet there it was. What kind of person sees a skull and decides, I'm gonna suck on that? What person is capable of this? Cake, that's who.

Walking through the airport, Larry was the physical embodiment of both defeat and depravity. He was more beaten and bruised than Josh had ever seen a person. He had a hard time even speaking, and through the periodic moans and groans, everything seemed sore. Josh says he actually saw parents pull their children closer as Larry walked past them in the airport.

"And that was the trip."

Josh finishes telling us the story. Our coffee is still warm, our cups mostly full. I shake it off and take a sip.

"You say he's never had sex before?"

Josh replies, "Not a virgin, but not experienced in the least bit. One, maybe two times previously, max. He's like twenty-seven years old."

"Experienced or not," I reply, "Does he not have any sense of self-preservation? Did he see a doctor or anything?"

Josh says, "Don't think he has yet, we just got back. You guys cannot tell him I told you this. He made me promise on the plane not to tell you, he's really embarrassed and likes you guys and doesn't want to scare you off, but I couldn't keep this to myself, I had to get this out."

It was at that point Josh reached that moment, where there's just nothing left to say, but you have to say *something*. The thing about the shrug is that it is hard to just let it play by itself. The *truth* lies in that shared understanding, where you can look at someone and they nod at you, and you nod back, and in that acknowledgement none yet all of the words are spoken, because you both know. It's not that you both know what happened exactly, but you know the truth that it represents. And that's enough.

The truth here was that our friend, who we had all had over to our house and shared meals and drinks with, our friend who had humbled himself to us and admitted he wasn't happy and asked us to support him in making a change, our friend who asked us to help him realize the life he aspired towards and to build some confidence and enjoy life's adventures and learn that sharing it with others had finally come out of his shell and just let the fuck loose, and did so in a way nobody could have predicted. Not by a long-shot.

We sat there for a minute, shaking our heads, eating do-nuts and sipping our coffees, still trying to comprehend exactly what Josh had just told us. Josh, still wading in the surreal stupor of having just witnessed it.

I throw it out there again, "Eight hours?"

Josh's eyes get wide and he nods, his face telling me to believe it. "I saw him. It was bad."

Another sip of coffee, "And he took Cake out to a steak dinner? That's different."

"I know."

"You don't normally go through the courtship process with a prostitute you met in a foreign country. That's like falling in love in the exact way you're not supposed to," I said.

Josh shakes his head and I continue, "I mean, senior chiefs and NCO's literally give that speech to their enlisted folks before weekend liberty, the don't fall in love at the strip club speech."

"He bought her a cake, too. Birthday gift."

"Because her name was Cake," says Nikki.

"Jesus." I take another sip of coffee.

"I'm dead serious, you guys can't let on that I told you, it'd be horrible for him."

"Don't worry, we won't," Nikki and I both say. Because really, what would it accomplish? It's not like telling him is somehow going to un-fuck Cake.

Thus began our months long shrug. We would go out with Larry numerous times after that, nobody mentioning anything, Larry completely unaware of what we had heard. When we asked him how the trip went, he said it was fun, wild times. What happens in Thailand stays in Thailand. That seemed like a sensible enough answer, and so life went on.

*　　　*　　　*

Thanksgiving rolled around and Larry, Nikki and I all wandered off to New Orleans to celebrate the holiday while Josh went back to Ohio for a few days. After the first night, Larry split from us and wandered off to choose his own misadventure, said he'd find a way home.

Not about to leave a fellow sailor behind, I asked him if he was sure, and he was adamant he'd be good to go, and that we shouldn't wait up for him. He gave us that look, and instinctively we knew it was the same look he gave Josh when he said he was going back for Cake. And like Josh, we knew we couldn't stop him.

Something in that look, the confidence, the determination. Something inside him throwing caution to the wind and embracing spontaneity. If he survived Thailand, he could survive anything.

Before we left New Orleans, I called him to make sure he was still good to go and had a way back to Pensacola, and he assured us he had arranged something. What left but to trust he had figured it out.

By the time Monday rolled around, he was back in formation as expected. This was the new Larry, fedora and all.

Things That Fascinate

The interesting thing about Larry and his misadventures in Thailand is how the story has aged over the years, and I chalk it up to being part of the beauty of storytelling. Like every story, with each retelling, it changes ever so slightly until its core truth becomes more and more evident over time. Through each retelling, it is both told and perceived through a different lens, revealing a little more through each iteration.

It went on for about six months, all of us putting on these Oscar worthy performances, embracing our little secret about his little secret. And yet our shrug begged to be addressed. You can't just keep it in.

It's the curiosity that gets you. You hear it once and it's like it opens a door, and you're only able to peer in from the outside. Just a peek, you can only see so much, just enough to light that flame. And because of our particular circumstance, the fact that we were sworn to secrecy – when there's nobody to ask who might be able to shed light on things, all you're left to do is to speculate. And as you speculate, your initial questions beget more questions, and you venture down detours that lead to even more unpredictable places.

Our own curiosities led us down rabbit holes of research, trying our best to learn what the procedures entailed and how it all worked. Starting with the basics, we didn't even know what the parts of a penis actually were or where erections came from. To us, a penis was always a penis, with a shaft and a head, and then there were the balls, not complicated. But Cake complicated things. We learned that nitric oxide is produced in the brain when you become sexually stimulated, and this nitric oxide stimulates an enzyme which causes the muscle cells in the penis to relax. Once relaxed, this allows the erectile tissue and blood vessels inside the penis to expand. When this happens, tissues called the corpora cavernosa and corpus spongiosum become compressed, which restricts the *outward* flow of blood. So now that there's more blood coming in than going out, that pressure causes an erection. This is where that old riff comes from that guys can't think when they're sporting a hard on, because there's not enough blood to operate their brains and their dicks at the same time. It's partially true, because an erect penis is literally filled with blood. There are no bones, and there's no muscle in the way you think about biceps or hamstrings. It's all carvernosa and spongiosum, which almost sound sexual just for the sake of sounding sexual.

With gender reassignment surgery, an incision is made in the penis and the skin is folded back on itself, allowing the testicles to be removed. What happens to all that cavernosa and spongiosum? It gets tucked away into the penis skin, which is reformed as the labia and clitoris. In the end, it pretty much looks like a vagina, just without the functionality.

Then there are the unusual phenomena, like phantom penises. It's the same effect as when an amputee is still getting used to the sensation of not having one of their limbs. They still have the sensation of having a limb where there is none because the brain hasn't made the adjustment yet. Same thing for losing a penis. You can still get stimulated, and when the blood starts flowing you may have the sensation that you're rock hard, but there's nothing there, it's just a vagina. This led to a whole host of other questions that never seemed to end.

Towards the end of that six-month stretch, Larry finally came clean to us in grand fashion. Josh gave us the warning. They were planning on coming over to our house for dinner and a few drinks, and Larry was going to drop the bomb, so we had to fake it.

It was surreal, the three of us sitting there, feigning surprise to his revealing of the legend of Cake. Larry and his Cakescapades. At least we could finally let up on our charade and finally ask him all the things we had only speculated about since Josh first opened that laptop.

Apart from the biological questions, the real questions that begged to be addressed were more situational. As it so happened, Larry had been keeping in touch with Cake via email and instant messenger. That's not something you normally see. Ladyboy status aside, Larry was essentially courting and maintaining a long-distance relationship with a Thai prostitute. Exactly what you're *not* supposed to do while on liberty. He was even considering bringing Cake to the states on a marriage visa like that 90 Day Fiancé show. How something like that would even play out is beyond imagination. "Sir, I need command sponsorship for someone I met in Thailand. Her name is Cake."

I've told this story numerous times over the years to a variety of people, and the reactions are sprawling. There's usually shock, that's pretty consistent. The eight-hour sex marathons, the wild disregard for his own health, the violence and grittiness of it all with his hair getting pulled out and the blood and shit covered sheets, it's all so depraved.

A lot of people simply can't get past the fact that Larry had sex with Cake, a ladyboy. They make leaps and bounds in logic, trying to ask the questions to reconcile it in their own minds. Questions like, was it basically like having anal sex with a guy? Was the oral sex like giving a blowjob? Is Larry gay? Of course, those questions are all missing the point. It couldn't have been like giving a blowjob because there was no penis – Cake was post-op. As for the anal sex, does it really matter? An anus is an anus, regardless of a person's sex. And as for Larry being gay, well again, it kind of misses the point – Larry wasn't hitting on the male bartender. He was hitting on someone who he perceived to be a woman. Cake was convincing, after all.

Those are only surface level questions about the real implications of the story. It takes a little more digging to get at the real truth of it. When you break it down, the real spectacle here is how Larry was at one polar end of the spectrum, the far end with basically *zero* experience, and through this wild sexual awakening, hooked up with someone who was at the complete opposite end of the spectrum, someone with *all* of the experience – sexual experience as both a man *and* a woman. And when you flush it out even more, you can argue that as it stands now, Larry is far more experienced sexually than most people will ever be in the entirety of their lifetimes. Ensign Larry, the former sheltered fat guy turned Naval Flight Officer turned sexual savant. Now *that* is revelatory.

*   *   *

It's this fascination with the perverse that drives so much of human curiosity. If it isn't researching gender reassignment surgery to better understand what your friend has been up to on vacation, it's lingering at the scene of a traffic accident or gawking at someone's house going up in flames. In the end you're just thankful it's not you who is experiencing it. Seeing some things through the eyes of others is a perfect substitution in some circumstances.

It all starts to connect, the absurd, the surreal, and the perverse. The absurd part is the deviation from what's expected, the surreal part is coming to terms with its truth, and the perverse is the part that keeps you looking at it. But there's a level of shame associated with the perverse, and it's built into our psyches. Even though objectively we know we don't want to look, it's taboo to admit that on that deeper level, we actually *do* want to keep looking. We *need* to keep looking to feed that curiosity, we *need* to dig further.

There's a reason we can't look away, and it's intrinsic in all of us. That's why gogo bars that feature ladyboys in Thailand exist, to satisfy that very real drive. If it didn't exist there, it would have to exist somewhere else. And to live it, to come to terms with it, to embrace it – it's all part of achieving a greater, more truthful understanding of that part of ourselves we'd rather not display for the world to see.

The most fascinating stories always tend to involve either sex, violence, bodily fluids, or some combination of all three. If not directly, you can usually find at least trace elements of one of those concepts at the heart of any great story. Some of those parallels are obvious, take for example a war story, where violence is usually the shock factor that drives the fascination, from which the viewer or reader or listener simply can't disengage. Stories about police chases and bank heists and drunken escapades all tap into those base themes to drive fascination. Even stories about the triumph of the human spirit somehow blend these elements. There has to be something to overcome, and raw human nature usually fuels that drive. At the very least, if physical violence is not the driving impetus, emotional violence can serve as a substitute.

These stories can spawn all manner of emotions and reactions. Take for example the story of a buddy who was having sex with his girlfriend, and it was such a wild and rollicking good time that at the end of it, it became so intense and orgasmic that he finally blew his load in the condom while still inside her. And at that moment of post-nut relaxation, when the blood flow finally shifted, his sphincter opened up and his diaphragm loosened and he let out a massive fart while still inside her. The look on both of their faces of surprise and shock and disgust. A moment of speechlessness. What happens now? She jumped off, grabbed her clothes, called him an asshole, and stormed into the bathroom while he burst into riotous laughter, lying on the bed with the used condom still attached to his slowly dying erection. The two have been married for over a decade.

Then there's the time Bermudez brought in a body on a felony warrant, as he was wont to do, which ultimately resulted in a hazmat scene.

Thing about Bermudez, he used to work for the postal service before joining the department. In delivering the mail for twenty years before becoming a cop, Bermudez got really good at recognizing faces and memorizing names. When he came on the job and started working Skid Row, he learned early on that he could study the felony warrant database page before his shift, see who was wanted, and then drive around the area and point out people he recognized from the page. It was like a street cop superpower. Working with Bermudez was like working with a human facial recognition machine, and when you worked with him, you knew you were going to get about three felony warrant arrests per night, easily.

A superpower like that is very much a double-edged sword. Because most people don't have Bermudez's superpower, they simply rely on finding reasons to stop people on the street based on them committing some kind of actual violation, and not just recognizing them from the warrant page. Then once they run them, if it turns out they have a warrant, great job, there's one in the tank.

The nice part about this is you get to be discerning with who you stop. Nobody in their right mind is going to stop someone who is covered in filth who would obviously be a nightmare to deal with, be it from the smell, having every medical issue known to man, or being plagued with something that might make *you* sick. The result is that people who fit this bill tend to never get stopped, so their warrants linger in the system for years.

But Bermudez would recognize them, and when he would see them and remember they had a warrant? Well, it is what it is. Now that he knew they were wanted on a felony, legally he had to take them. As a result, Bermudez tended to bring in people who were just the absolute worst. We called them "Bermudez bodies."

One night I remember Gina and I had just come back to the station to work on some admin, and were making our way back to the detective offices. As we passed by the report writing room, we could hear someone moaning and calling for help, like someone was in pain. I peek into the room, which is completely empty except for one person locked in the holding tank. He's doubled over, grasping his torso.

"I need help, it hurts so much!"

"What's wrong, what is it?" I ask him.

"My stomach, I can't hold it, it hurts so much! I need an ambulance!"

I go over the radio and request an RA (rescue ambulance) for him, "1FB24, requesting an RA for a male, forty years of age, conscious and breathing, complaining of severe pain to the torso, Central report writing room."

I stand by with the guy and ask Gina to find his arresting officer. As she wanders off to find whose guy this is, I let him know an ambulance is on its way and I try to calm him down, offering what little assurance I can that they're going to get him some help.

Without warning, the man makes his way to his feet, pulls his pants down to his ankles, drops to a squatting position, and begins shitting neon green liquid directly onto the floor.

His asshole is literally like a fire hydrant, the pressure of the blast knocking him to his knees as the liquid spews out his ass and up and onto the walls of the room, the plexiglass, everywhere.

And it's literally neon green, like the color of a reflective traffic vest or the green M&M, depending on the lighting.

It looks like the scene from Men in Black when Will Smith and Tommy Lee Jones blast the alien apart in the desert and bluish green goo sprays everywhere. Except here, it's in a small holding tank and the smell is beyond rancid.

Gina wanders back in alongside Bermudez, who just so happens to be the guy who arrested him. Both of them run up to me as I stand there in shock, unable to look away.

"What is happening, what'd he do?"

"He just started shitting everywhere, I don't know! Who did you bring in, Bermudez?!"

Bermudez shakes his head in amazement, "He was fine when we jammed him, he didn't look sick or anything."

At least he wouldn't have to transport the guy – the ambulance would handle that part. Turns out the guy had full blown AIDS and the medicine he was taking did a real number on his digestive tract which is what caused the neon green shitstorm, who knew.

When paramedics finally arrived, they were both shocked and appalled. Worst hospital transport of their lives. The watch commander had Bermudez seal off the tank with yellow tape – off fucking limits, do not touch. They put in a call to facilities maintenance. When the janitorial guy got there, he took one look and walked away. They ended up calling the hazmat team to come and do the cleanup.

The strange part is that in the moments between when the guy finally left and when the cleanup crew arrived, every officer who passed by couldn't resist the urge to pull out their phone and take a picture of the green, shitty cell. Who anybody would show such a picture to is anyone's best guess, but something like that deserved to be enshrined, if for nothing more than posterity.

Sometimes the fascination is driven by the perverse, which doesn't always have to mean sex. Take a good horror story. Why do people gravitate to the horror genre? It taps into a deep-seated desire to experience in a safe way what would otherwise be dangerous, through some modality of violence while at the same time through the perversion of our logical senses, the supernatural.

Wilmington Cemetery lies at the intersection of east O St. and Eubank Ave. in Wilmington, CA. Wilmington is a neighborhood in south Los Angeles within the LAPD's jurisdiction, located in Harbor Division. After leaving Central I transferred to Harbor because it was closer to home, and after so much time spent in Skid Row, I was about ready for a change.

I had been working Harbor for a bit over two years and had passed by the cemetery numerous times, not thinking anything of it. I had never gotten any calls there and it was fairly unremarkable. Little did I know, the house at the end of O St. which bordered the graveyard was haunted.

Story goes, it's early evening around 7pm when the call comes out. It's getting dark outside, but there's a small bit of daylight left. Nothing unusual about the month or day or

147

hour. Only thing unusual are the comments of the call, which at first sound like nothing more than a typical domestic disturbance. The RTO broadcasts that there's several members of a family outside arguing loudly and fighting on their front lawn and it's spilling into the street. See comments for additional.

Every unit who scrolls through on their mobile computer reads on and sees something that catches their eye, a blurb that reads "Possible supernatural occurrences involved."

Now every cop in the division who isn't doing anything is enroute to see what the big deal is. On one hand, they've all been around the block and have seen everything, but they've never been to a call with *supernatural* circumstances, whatever that means. Probably a big nothing, but worth checking out anyway.

When the first unit arrives, they immediately begin sizing up the scene. It's just as the call describes, there's an entire family out front, yelling loudly at one another. They're an old school Hispanic family and it's all in Spanish. They're all directing their anger towards the teenage girl, who stands separated and ostracized from the rest of them. Shouts and accusations going back and forth between everyone, mainly accusing each other of whose fault it is that she did whatever it is she did to set everyone off. The only real consistent thing is that whatever it is, it's her fault.

More units start arriving and approaching the family, trying to calm everyone down and help the primary unit get to the bottom of what's happening. It's all chaotic, tears are flowing, and the curses and yelling are drowning out the approaching police sirens. Who knows what happened, maybe the girl got knocked up and now the family's in turmoil? Wouldn't be the first time.

Then the mother and the father and the grandma all start accusing her and pointing, "Ella está mala, mala bruja diabla!" Translates roughly to she's bad, a bad witchy devil girl. They say the spirit is punishing them all for her wickedness. None of them want to go back inside, not with her. Whatever demonic possession there is, it wants her out of the house.

Of course, these cops are all rolling their eyes. Now they've seen everything. Short of a crime, there's nothing for them to do other than warn everybody to quiet down and stop bothering their neighbors. Just go back inside, sort out your issues in the privacy of your own walls.

But they're refusing to go back in with the girl, they just won't let her back in. And the family is pleading with these guys, begging them to believe their story. Just go inside and see for yourself, the place is trashed. Take the girl with you, you'll see what happens, it doesn't want her in there anymore.

Supervisor arrives on scene and tries to get his head around the commotion. Primary unit tells him what's going on, and they all finally give in and decide to walk inside and take a look around with the girl, just to appease everyone.

The family is beyond thankful, finally someone who is willing to help. And they're straight up terrified, nobody's seen a family act like this, and these guys are a bunch of south end cops. They've been through the shit yet this is the first time they've ever seen a family terrified to go back inside their own house because of a so-called "spirit" being upset with their daughter.

The guys make their way inside. It's around dusk, so just a little bit of light is making its way into the partially drawn living room windows. Just like they said, the place is trashed. Looks like a tornado just ripped through the living room. Books and trinkets are knocked off shelves, broken dishes and lamps and spilled food litter the carpet, with broken glass everywhere and picture frames knocked off kilter. It's the two patrol guys who are the primary unit who went in alongside the supervisor. The others are waiting outside with the rest of the family. The girl is right next to them, looking sheepish and guilty.

"Ok so now what?" one of the officers says to the girl.

Suddenly, a King James Version Holy Bible levitates off the dining room table and flies across the living room through the air and cracks the girl in the face. She falls back on her ass and the color in these guys' faces just vanishes, they go completely stone cold white. They stumble back, losing their balance as they help the girl back to her feet, barking out to no one in particular, "What the fuck was that? Did you see that?"

They rush out the house back towards the rest of the family standing by with their confused partners by the curb amidst the staggered police cars, waiting for an answer. The supervisor composes himself ever so slightly, his face still white like he'd literally seen a ghost.

He declares to the family, "There's no crime here, this isn't a police matter, we are leaving. Call us if there's a crime."

And just like that he signals to everyone to get in their cars and take off.

He says to the guys who went in with him, "Meet me back at the station." They're just as spooked as he is.

When the supervisor gets back to the station, he tells the two cops to dock their body worn video cameras, except they've already done it, they're a step ahead of him.

He walks into the watch commander's office and sits in front of a computer and begins logging in. The watch commander asks him, "What the hell's going on, Mike? You go to that call on O?"

He doesn't answer directly, kind of stumbles over his own words and barely manages to spit out, "I need to see our videos, I just need to see the videos, I don't know."

The two coppers rush into the office and post up behind the boss, all staring eagerly at the screen, waiting for the video to play. Once it finally loads, it's too dark to make out much detail but you can hear everything. You can see and make out the general scene but you can't see the Bible levitate from anywhere. It's super shaky because these guys have their cameras mounted on their chests and they're moving around. All you can see is something small zip across the screen towards the girl, but you can't make out what it is or where it came from. Then she loses her balance, the camera starts shaking even more as they begin scrambling, and you can hear it all, the shuffling as they try to help her up, the cursing, the questions, trying to confirm if they saw what they saw.

"What happened?" the watch commander asks, "What was it?"

Stories about that particular house are known throughout the supernatural investigation community. Do a few searches on some of the more popular podcasts for the San

Pedro haunted house and you'll be dazzled with tales of the different families who have rented the place out and been driven from it by demonic forces.

Within the division, at least amongst the guys who have been there for awhile, they'll tell you about its magnetic draw to the surreal. There usually aren't any calls there, but when there are, they tend to be strange.

Some people have claimed to see a woman in a rocking chair through the upstairs window that faces the cemetery, but the families always said there was no old woman who lived there, and there's no rocking chair in the house. Nobody even goes into the upstairs room, it's just an attic. Scarier because the house simply looks haunted, even from the outside. It's just old. I guess the owners of haunted houses don't appreciate a good contractor.

In the days following the incident, that supervisor was a bit out of it. He came into work, went to his calls, but was distracted. Last anybody spoke to him about it he was trying to track down a priest to ask some questions, but nobody knows what he was told. Every time he's asked about it, his face goes kind of white again and he answers really briefly, "Yeah. No explanation, I don't know. Fucking weird." That feeling when there just aren't any words to express it. It's as if it's too perverse to actually speak.

*   *   *

Some years later I was catching up with Josh and we got to talking about Larry. Larry had no doubt found himself in some misadventures in the years since we lost touch. When he checked into NAS Oceana in Virginia, he started dating this local girl who lived in the ghetto part of town. I never met her and I'm sure she was a decent girl, but picturing Larry it just came off as bizarre, yet somehow fitting.

After moving into their own place together, Larry was shocked when a SWAT team suddenly kicked in his door and rousted him from bed and placed him under arrest on a narcotics charge, of all things. Turns out, the house he had just moved into used to be occupied by a notorious meth dealer who happened to resemble Larry.

There's Larry, pleading with the heavily armed SWAT guy, "No I'm a fighter pilot, I'm in the Navy, I swear, I just moved in!"

The SWAT guy looking at Larry, then at the picture on the rap sheet, then back to Larry, then back to the rap sheet...when the commander got a call that night, they had to vouch for the fact that Larry had just checked into the squadron and couldn't have established such an illustrious meth dealing career in such a short period of time. They eventually apologized and let him go.

Larry began having migraines and blacked out one day while driving home from base and crashed his car into a ditch. He ultimately ended up ok, but it killed his flying career. Can't have a guy flying around pulling g's who gets migraines.

The Navy determined the cause of his migraines was related to the flying itself, so Larry hit the jackpot with a medical retirement from the Navy as a Lieutenant Junior Grade. Every 15th and 30th of the month for the rest of his life he gets a regular paycheck from Uncle Sam. Ensign Larry, who had his Cake and ate it too, living the comp life, albeit with a few headaches from time to time.

Larry's ghetto-girl relationship didn't last long. He managed to meet a girl in Thailand on a subsequent trip named Bun Ma – of course, Larry couldn't pronounce it correctly, so he said it in that weird hybrid Jamaican Thai accent he had developed in an effort to be more worldly – "Boon-maaa." Like grandma and grandpa and boonma and boonpa.

Bun Ma was very traditional. She came from a lower middle-class family who owned a small plot of land in rural Thailand, and the prospect of marrying an American was a ticket to ensuring a very prosperous future. But that wasn't her only way out, because Bun Ma was smart enough and fortunate enough to have gotten a college education too.

After she moved to the states with Larry, she took over management of a fast food joint in his hometown. And even with her professional and educational background, she still embraced her cultural conservatism. Every morning before work, she'd wake up at the crack of dawn and prepare breakfast for her husband from scratch. She'd clean up after him, clean the house, do his laundry, and prepare dinner for the evening. Somehow Larry had found a woman who was both smart and willing to look after him, all while pulling a tax-free government pension. And all by the age of thirty. It's like he found the cheat codes to life.

Josh and I had a good laugh and finished our drinks. Leave it to Larry to bring the entertainment. Some weeks later I learned that Cake had died in Germany. It came as a shock as Josh relayed the news. Why was Cake in Germany? How did she die? Does Cake have family, will anyone be at the funeral?

As all these thoughts raced through my mind, I raced to the next steps of seeing how expensive flights to Germany were. That's what Cake had become even though I had never met her, a colorful central character and a center of gravity to our collective experiences, if only by proxy.

Truthful storytelling has the ability to fuse the absurd with the surreal and the perverse, and to burrow deep into our psyches, becoming a part of our very makeups in the process. Come to find out that Cake had actually died two years prior. That same sense of loss and emptiness trickled through my mind in the same way that it did with Chukums, realizing her memory would be lost except through those few people she came to live in through her story. Like Chukums, Cake was destined for her own 5th and San Julian, and through her it felt like a part of us was headed there too. Cake had died and we weren't even there to mourn.

We don't know how it happened. Probably an overdose, but no way to know for sure. And then the mind begins to wander some more. How did Josh find out that Cake died? Was Larry keeping in touch with Cake? Was someone keeping in touch with Cake's family? Did Larry's wife Bun Ma even know about Cake? Did she have any idea about Larry's sordid past? The questions never seemed to end.

Cake may be gone, but her story is still very much alive. The story is the same, but it lives and breathes and evolves with every retelling. And with each retelling, its truth becomes ever clearer, begging to achieve that ever elusive shrug.

That Wasn't Funny

Taking a look into the perverse and the depraved can sometimes generate surprising reactions. It's like how when you catch yourself laughing at something that in actuality, you know shouldn't be funny, but you can't help but laugh anyway. Like catching yourself laughing at a funeral, or when someone slips and falls, or at words like *buttfuck* or *dickclown*.

When I was about twelve, I had my first sex-ed class. For a bunch of sixth graders, sex-ed class was a big deal. And when I say a big deal, I mean it was a *big* deal. Before the class even began, we had to get permission slips, *just for a class.* And if any parents objected, their kid could be pulled out and sent to a non-sex-ed class for the time being to learn about nutrition. I guess it was so they could at least be healthy while being more clueless than the rest of their peers. Of course, this would have carried a much worse social stigma than any STD ever could have wrought. Jimmy didn't learn about sex! Maybe Jimmy should go fuck himself…

It was such a childhood evolution, sex-ed. The big anticipation for a bunch of eleven-year-olds was waiting eagerly for sixth grade, because that's when you finally got to have a locker, and there were *school dances*. It would be just like Boy Meets World or The Fresh Prince of Bel Air or Saved by The Bell. The possibilities were endless.

We may have been dorks in fifth grade, but just you wait til sixth grade and all that shit was gonna change. The anticipation of being able to decorate our lockers with pictures of swimsuit models and finally being able to ask Lauren Petrelli to the dance, it was almost too much.

Then there was *slow dancing*. Just wait for that goddamn *slow dancing*. In no time we'd be having *sex*, whatever the hell that actually was – we'd be raising families, running businesses and storming battlefields and all the myriad other adventures adulthood carried. And it all started with those dances. That curiosity starts at a young age, and never quite dies.

Interesting thing about sex-ed class was that it butted right up against summer break. I guess the thinking was that there were all these horned up twelve-year-olds about to graduate the sixth grade, and now that their pheromones had been activated because of all the dancing, they wouldn't be able to keep their hands off each other if released into the wild, so they'd better teach em before it was too late.

Imagine the absurdity of a bunch of seventh grade girls, all impregnated by boys who were laughing at words like *buttfuck* and *dickclown*. Just imagine it.

They pre-briefed us on the expectations, primarily that we would exemplify a level of maturity and appropriateness, because sex is a serious and delicate subject.

Hell yeah, we've been dancing all year and now we were gonna learn about sex. We can be appropriate, we're gonna be appropriate as fuck.

No laughing. Teacher doesn't want to hear any laughing, no "ewww's" or "ahhhh's" or giggling or gasping because we're old enough to know better.

You know, like the mature twelve-year-olds that we were.

We were going to be hearing words like penis, vagina, and breasts. Those are just parts of the human body and there's no need to be awkward about it. Got it, no awkwardness, all on board, awesome. Boobies. We're ready.

One of the next things they did is put on a video. When I was a kid it was a bit more slickly produced than what you imagine the sex-ed videos back in the 1950's would have been, the ones that really delved into the whole duck and cover thing – not because a Russian nuclear attack would kill you, but because the clap and an unpredictable vagina might.

No, the videos change with the times. Our video was produced probably sometime around 1995. One segment I remember was the interview segment. They had a bunch of different cutaways of young teens being interviewed about their first experiences with sexual attraction, boys getting hard-ons at inopportune times, girls having awkward first periods. Legit funny stuff, all told with smiles and light-hearted comedic music accents playing in the background, all meant to convey a sense of normalcy and ease. They didn't want to scare us, they wanted us to embrace the fact that that soon, we too would be the ones having these experiences that we'd be looking back on with smiles and blushes and silly embarrassment.

One girl in particular relayed a story about her dad having to take her to the store to pick up maxi-pads and tampons on a weekend when her mom was away on business – a super progressive idea for 1995 – which somehow turned into an embarrassing excursion to a lingerie store to buy her a training bra. Her timing and delivery were impeccable.

In my defense, the story was obviously intended to be funny, so who was I not to laugh at what amounted to an expertly crafted standup bit? I let out a refined chuckle, as only such a polished twelve-year-old as I could, which pierced the room of my shocked classmates and disappointed teacher.

Come on guys, it was a joke, it was *supposed* to be a joke. Surely, it's ok to laugh at an obvious joke, right?

But amidst all the dirty looks, I had to hang my head in shame. I wasn't supposed to be laughing, they specifically told us not to. This was *sex-ed* class, the one you had to get a *permission slip* for.

The look of scorn from the teacher said it all – I thought you were one of the trailblazers Chris, one of the mature ones. Why did it have to be you…

There is most definitely a link between laughter and the absurd. One of the theories as to the cause of humor and why we laugh comes from that of German philosopher Immanuel Kant. Without getting into the finer details and nuances of the philosophy, Kant came up with what would eventually be dubbed "Incongruity Theory," the idea that humor arises when our expectation of the world *as it ought to be* is violated with a reality incongruous to that expectation, and that laughter is the body's natural reaction. True absurdity takes form the moment that realization dissolves into nothingness, and all that's left is the reaction. It's the moment we realize there is no greater significance to any of it, no rhyme or reason, and the coming to terms with it just vanishes. Absent any perceived harm, all that's left is to laugh.

Think to most standup comedians and how they formulate jokes. The set-up, whether it's an entire act or only a few lines, serves to establish that very expectation. The punchline is when that expectation is violated and the audience laughs. The comic nature of it expresses a fundamental truth of that absurdity – since there is nothing left to say and there's nothing left to think about and there's nothing left to rationalize – what more can you do other than accept it? You laugh it away. You can extend this concept to most any form of comedy or humor – knock knock jokes, one-liners, puns, witticisms, slapstick – it all applies.

The same holds true for tragedy. There's the old saying that tragedy is the root of all comedy. One could argue that tragedy and comedy are one in the same, the result of the same incongruity, the only difference being that one is associated with some form of suffering and the other is ultimately harmless. It's why we laugh at something like the Wet Bandits in Home Alone as they are pummeled by a nine-year-old. The expectation is that these grown men will no doubt kidnap and probably murder the child, but the reality is that *they* are the ones who are bested by him. It's the absurd part that makes it funny.

The interesting thing is how we laugh at the manner in which they are absolutely owned by the kid, taking full paint cans to the face, grabbing hot door handles, slipping on ice and cracking their heads. Its humor comes from the absurdity and the fact that it is obviously harmless, simply because they are so overexaggerated in their reactions to being beaten senseless, and they get back up every time.

It would be markedly a bit more tragic if it was played for realism, because it would be less deviant from an established expectation – a brick to the head thrown from the roof of a New York brownstone would kill you. There might be a subtle sense of dark humor on some level as it's still a child who is doing it, but it's like a seesaw – add a little realism, lose a little levity.

Fran Lebowitz was once quoted as saying, "I don't want to die in a way people find amusing." Because who would? The amusement arises from the incongruity which is rooted in the absurd. And nobody wants to view their life, or their death, for that matter, as absurd.

"Poor Austin, he choked to death on a baloney sandwich."

"Baloney? I thought he was vegan?"

"I read the autopsy, baloney and mayonnaise."

"Gross."

One of my fears is dying in a freak accident due to my own stupidity. I feel so sorry for all those Florida men, those Darwin award recipients, whose families had to bury them with the knowledge that they died doing something most children would know better than to do. Joe Exotic's meth addicted boyfriend Travis wanted to demonstrate that a Ruger pistol, even with a bullet in the chamber, wouldn't fire without the magazine properly inserted in the gun. So he put the magazine-less pistol up to his head and pulled the trigger. Boom. And that was that. Tragic, yet people laughed because it was so goddamn ridiculous. Imagine witnessing something like that, an absolute moment of truth, where you are literally left speechless. Nothing left to say, except that a Ruger will in fact fire without an inserted magazine.

*　　　*　　　*

There is a series of sleeping disorders commonly referred to as parasomnias. They include things like sleepwalking, sleep paralysis, narcolepsy, sleep-talking – think any neurological affliction that might make getting a peaceful night's sleep difficult. They're mostly harmless in and of themselves, but depending on circumstances and a person's surroundings, they can be dangerous under certain conditions.

There have been multiple documented instances of people committing murders while sleepwalking. Defense attorneys have tried to use sleepwalking as a defense, though usually unsuccessfully. They try to establish there was no motive or intent for the person to have committed the crime, because generally a person has to be aware of their own actions, if they in fact *intended* to do them.

You start to wade into tricky waters when you talk about intent, because you venture towards questions like, is a person who is under the influence of alcohol, or maybe a hallucinogenic like LSD, really in control of their own cognition? When it comes to sex, you technically can't consent if you're under the influence – think the date rape drug, roofies. A person didn't say no because they couldn't say no, because their decision-making capacity was inhibited. Therefore, there was no consent, ergo they are a victim.

But is there any kind of parallel if you committed a crime? This thinking leads you down the path to the idea that maybe the intent transferred from one action to the other if a person willingly took the cognition altering substance. "I was drunk" is an easy enough get out of jail free card if all you did was say something that people perceived as being a little offensive. You can play it off that you didn't *really* mean it and you can apologize and try to make amends. This doesn't really apply if you just killed someone.

But then you can talk it in circles even more, because if your intent transferred when you got drunk and committed the crime, then didn't the victim who got drunk imply consent in that same manner when they didn't say no? Of course not, that's victim blaming – and around and around it goes.

Intent, motive, cognition, awareness – nothing's easy when it comes to these ideas because the processes of logic and reason lead you in these twisting circles, and eventually you get to a point where the inevitable conclusions are wildly inconsistent with where your moral compass and common sense tell you where you need to be. After all, you can't equate the experience of a sexual assault victim with that of a murderer. Those are obviously two very different things, with the subtle difference being that in one scenario you're affecting the world around you, whereas in the other the world is affecting you – i.e. perpetrator versus victim. As a concept, it's a frighteningly small distinction, but it really is everything.

Cognition and awareness definitely play into it, the idea of actively doing something. Otherwise, it's just an accident, an unfortunate circumstance beyond a person's control.

Like the insanity plea. The insanity plea has been used much more successfully than sleepwalking as a defense, but it's the same principle at play.

At least with insanity, there's an easier case to be made. A person can have a documented history of medical diagnosis and treatments. They likely have prescription medication, and if it can be proven they were undermedicated at the time, then you can make an argument they simply had an episode beyond their control. But sleepwalking? It's a lot harder to establish that baseline. Because sleepwalking or other parasomnias tend to be harmless, why go through the trouble of documenting them in the first place?

On the flip side, an insanity plea and associated ruling is not a get out of jail free card either. When it's determined a person is not competent to stand trial, or if they are ruled "not guilty" by way of insanity, the court usually imposes a handful of other legal requirements, namely that the person be hospitalized until they are competent to stand trial, otherwise until forever. It's a sentence without being a sentence, but it's not a conviction either. Remember how the justice system works in mysterious ways?

The other thing about sleepwalking cases is that it so often surprises the person who did the act. When they finally wake up, when they come to, they suddenly find themselves staring at a horrific crime scene with no recollection of how any of it came to pass. What's a person to do? Try to fix things? Instinct says to try and hide the evidence because you might have fucked up ever so slightly, by you know, murdering someone.

Anyone experiencing that much shock, they're not going to have the presence of mind to simply call the police and report that they just accidentally murdered someone while they were sleepwalking – they'd have to be a special brand of crazy to do something like that. This logic leads them to basically seal their own fate by making themselves look even more guilty by trying to cover it up, even though they don't even remember doing what they did. There's a legal term for that – it's called "Consciousness of Guilt," and it's often used to establish intent, even though this type of evidence frequently tends to be circumstantial.

Now I never murdered or assaulted my wife, but I had been married for about six months when I had my first night terror.

We were living in Pensacola and I was in aviation pre-flight training. We had just gotten down to Florida, excited to be starting on this new adventure as a couple. We had just finished having a bunch of furniture delivered to our apartment, had just set up our new bedframe, and bought a bunch of new much needed cookware. I was making good money and Nikki had just accepted a job offer at the local spa. This was all before Larry and his shenanigans. Things were smooth sailing.

One night it's about 2am, we're both fast asleep. I'm having this dream. I'm sitting in a living room, or maybe it's a study or a library. It looks like Masterpiece Theater, with an old school Victorian feel. There's a fireplace hosting a few burning logs, the embers shooting up and creating a cascade of dancing shadows across the room, warming me as I sit next to a bookshelf with a dozen classically bound books.

Portrait paintings adorn the walls, paintings of lords and duchesses, illuminated by the relaxing orange glow of the fire. It's calming, peaceful. I'm sitting in a grand chair that feels like a cushioned throne. I'm sitting deep in the chair, all the way back. It's wildly oversized and I feel almost like a child with my feet dangling off the edge.

I'm sipping a cup of hot cocoa. And it's the most delicious, the most sultry goddamn cup of hot cocoa I've ever had. It's level five. In this dream world, the measurement of hot cocoa comes in levels, and this is most definitely level five, the high-end stuff – the fanciest, the richest, the finest of all the cocoas. Every time I sip it, I can literally taste how wonderful it is, and I close my eyes and I'm transported within the dream to an even more euphoric state of bliss. It's the most perfect scene. It's probably snowing outside, but I can't even be bothered to look because it's so comfy and warm and perfect and it doesn't even matter. And that cocoa is piping hot, absolutely warming my insides. This stuff really is level five – life is level five, and this is heaven.

As I'm lost in the bliss of the level five hot chocolate, I become slightly cognizant of people walking past me at spaced intervals. They're older men and they're wearing white lab coats. They're walking from a back room at the end of a dark hallway past me to the front door and out into the world. They aren't too distracting, but they are noticeable. It doesn't matter, they can't pull me away from my little slice of heaven.

Until I notice two of them struggling to walk down the hallway. They appear to be carrying something, or someone. As I look a little closer in between sips, I see they are carrying what appears to be a limp body. One of the men is holding the body under the armpits with the arms dangling and the fingertips barely scraping the ground. The other is situated on the other end between the legs, carrying it at the joints of the knees. The man holding the knees is walking backwards down the hallway as they make their way towards me.

Are they taking the body out the front door? They move slowly, delicately, trying their best not to bump into the walls of the narrow corridor. There's very little light to guide them – the fireplace is the only illuminating source. As they near me, I make out that it's not a human body. No, it's a puppet. A marionette puppet. A wooden dummy, like Pinocchio. Why are they carrying a puppet as if it was a dead person?

They're about to pass me when suddenly the puppet begins to thrash wildly, and the men struggle to keep it under control. And they're only a few feet from me, and I'm trapped because I'm sitting so deep in the chair and the level five hot chocolate is so hot and my hands are occupied and I can't push it away or defend myself or get up and move because the chair is too big and I'm about to scream because there's nothing else for me to do –

Suddenly I'm awakened by a light touch – my wife is shaking me, trying to usher me awake.

"Honey, wake up, wake up! You're having a nightmare!"

I'm startled awake and I find myself in my bedroom. My heart is racing, but everything is just as normal as when I drifted off. I'm safe, my wife is there.

"Sorry, thanks. Goodnight."

She drifts back to sleep and I turn in the covers. I reach over and hold her, feeling the warmth of her body against mine. What an odd dream. I had apparently been moaning, muttering indecipherably. Loud enough to have woken her, at the very least.

As I drift back to sleep, I find my way back to that same scene. I'm back in the chair, and the warmth of the fireplace is so inviting, it's such a narcotic feeling. The chocolate, so sweet, so rich, so strong. Level five. Piping hot. So hot I have to hold the cup with both hands. I've never done drugs, I've never injected heroin, but this must be the feeling you get when you shoot up. If this is what it's like, why would anyone ever want to experience anything else? It's so pacifying, so relaxing, to just drift in the smoothness of the feeling.

I take in the scene, the grandeur of it all, admiring its sophistication. Maybe someday *I* will be one the dukes or lords enshrined on the walls of the manor, watching over its glorious splendor. There are no longer any men in lab coats wandering up and down the hallway. So much more relaxing, to be rid of the distraction.

I make a passing glance down the hallway, and as I look back towards the fireplace, I suddenly return to the hallway with a double take. It looked as if there was a person peeking out from a room at the end of the hall. Is there someone there? It's empty now. Maybe my eyes are playing tricks on me, I'm so enamored in the moment.

I start to turn away, then a small head peeps out again. I snap my gaze to the hallway and the head ducks back into the room. There is definitely someone there, like they're playing peek-a-boo.

Tension starts to rise in my stomach. It's a feeling of unease, something's not right.

Suddenly a small framed figure leaps out from the room and starts bolting down the hallway, directly for me. It's another goddamn puppet.

And as it sprints towards me, at the last moment it leaps directly at me with outstretched arms and with a look of menace in its wooden eyes and its snarling teeth and my hands are holding the hot chocolate so they're occupied and I can't fight it off and I'm so deep in the seat and I don't have time to move and I'm gonna spill the hot drink everywhere and burn myself and there's nothing left to do but scream –

I wake up screaming at the top of my lungs, struck with absolute terror. Nikki springs awake, sits bolt upright in the bed trying to orient herself. And just as soon as I'm jousted violently awake, I break into laughter. Did I really just have a night terror about a marionette puppet sprinting at me? It's so absurd, it's so ridiculous. I'm laughing hysterically, but Nikki doesn't find it funny in the least. Poor girl, she was sleeping peacefully and was startled awake by what she believed to be someone breaking into the house and trying to kill her husband. She'd never heard me scream before. This was a first. This was a shocking first.

Six months we had been married, and considering I had been away at OCS for four of those months, we were effectively two months into marriage. How is it that *now* I would suddenly develop night terrors? Seemingly out of the blue. Imagine if she had known about this before. I wonder if she was suddenly having buyer's remorse, if this was what marriage was going to be like...

It turned out to be a fairly regular thing. Our marriage, plagued by a series of bizarre, episodic night terrors. A few months would go by and sure enough I'd tell her, "Honey it's been a few months, I'm due."

And it'd never fail. Fast forward a few nights, maybe a week goes by, and I'd wake up in a screaming fit, frightening both myself and her awake in the middle of the night. And just like that first time, I'd break into uncontrollable laughter. And also, just like that first time, she'd get just as angry.

It never stopped being funny for me. I wouldn't always remember the substance of the dreams – they weren't all memorable or so realistically vivid. But more often than not, they would be absolutely ridiculous.

I started exploring the common themes, and the one commonality in all of them involved me not being in control. More so, it would be about me somehow *losing* control. I would have my hands occupied, like with the hot chocolate. Or I would be carrying a large box while being attacked.

And it's not just the concept of my hands being occupied. In one particular dream, I was living out the plot of the movie Inception. I was deep within my own dream, and delving into someone else's dream. Two dream levels down. While me and a team of dream extractors were deep into the dream world, we were sitting at a breakfast table with the target. And a little voice in my head kept telling me, *you're in his dream – stop drawing attention to the inconsistencies.* You know, like in the movie. And I would look at a detail. Then another detail. And then it started to spiral in a series of thought associations. I'm eating a breakfast burrito, breakfast burritos have eggs, eggs come out of chickens' butts, what if something is coming out of my butt, what if it's an egg coming out of my butt, oh my God a whole burrito is coming out of my butt, oh my God it's all collapsing – and I wake up screaming. Losing total control, laughing like a maniac while my wife angrily storms out the bedroom.

"But honey, there was a burrito coming out of my ass!"

"I don't care!"

This is marriage.

In the years since that first night terror, we've made adjustments. Really, she's the one who has made the adjustments. Now she usually doesn't even wake me up anymore – she just lets me ride it out. It's become such a regular thing, she just comes to expect it every few months or so, when she knows "I'm due."

Usually, it'll start with the moaning and she may nudge me a couple times, but if that doesn't do the trick, oh well. She figures if I start screaming, I'll just wake myself up and laugh it off anyway, so why bother breaking herself out of a deep sleep?

It usually works out that way, but the risk is that the dream becomes so vivid and I *don't* wake myself up, and instead start grabbing at her or thrashing wildly in bed. It's happened a couple times, but those instances are few and far between. And even with those, it's hard not to laugh, at least on my end.

It's all part of a long history I have of laughing at the wrong time, or at the very least, at inappropriate times. First time I gave my wife a taste of this we had been dating for about a month or so. We were getting more and more comfortable with each other, so I decided to escalate our relationship – I was going to scare her. Prank time.

I waited until we were having a night in. We're watching a movie at her place, it's a super romantic evening, good mood, getting good vibes.

I wait until she gets up and goes over to the bathroom. When she closes the door, I sneak over to the doorway and sit on the floor just outside. My plan is simple, not complicated in the least. It'll be a good, quick, honest scare.

When she comes out the bathroom, I'll grab her ankle and make a sharp barking noise or something – it'll be hilarious, she won't expect anything. I'm expecting her to jump and let out a scream, then she'll slap me playfully, and then hopefully that play-fighting turns flirtatious, and then that leads into some more nudging and tickling, and then that'll lead into some so and so, and then that'll lead into some yada yada yada…should make for a good evening.

She comes out after a minute. I'm set up, and I spring my brilliant plan. She screams, jumps, and then starts crying and clutches her chest.

This plan is backfiring fast. There's no playful slapping or nudging, definitely no tickling. I'm laughing at first, but then when I realize she's crying, it isn't funny anymore. It isn't funny at all. This is the exact opposite of funny. I really biffed this one, there isn't going to be any so and so, and there definitely isn't going to be any yada yada yada.

I apologize and apologize, and I hold her and rub her back and ask her if I can get her anything. I'm feeling like a complete moron, probably because I am. Through tears, she asks me, "Why would you do that?!"

I look down with a stupid expression on my face. Shameful, clueless, wrong. Couldn't have been any more wronger. Nothing to say but the one phrase that would come to piss her off more than any other thing I've ever said to her.

"Umm…I thought it would be funny."

That phrase, that singular phrase, packs so much power in terms of the absurdity it implies.

172

I thought it would be funny.

It's absurdity in action, almost by definition. If absurdity is the deviation from expectation, what better example of that deviation than the expectation of a funny prank which turns out to be so incredibly misguided? Something that was supposed to be funny, but turned out to be the exact opposite of funny.

One of the worst cases I've ever seen of "I thought it would be funny" happened to an unknown police officer who worked Central Division. I don't know who it was or when it happened, but it most definitely has to be true because it's left such a lasting impression, it's formed a whole worldview. Not just for me, but for almost every cop who's worked the division. It's gone so far as to dictate the tactics that Central cops use when interacting with the local population. It's cemented itself in the minds and memories of hundreds of officers who have passed through Skid Row. Some people may claim to have known the guy who did it or the guy it happened to, but really it could have been anyone. That's the magic of how true it is.

Legend has it that there was once a criminal on Skid Row. Nobody knows who this guy was or what he did. Nobody knows if he was white or black or Hispanic or Asian or anything else. Nobody knows how tall he was, how much he weighed, or how long he'd been out on the streets. Nobody can tell you if he was on parole, if he was a junkie or a crackhead. Nobody can even tell you if he had much of a criminal record. Was he on drugs? Maybe. Maybe not. Probably? Nobody knows for sure.

These are all facts nobody can confirm, although we can make some educated inferences. But what makes it scary is the simple fact that we *don't* know. There's no way we can, because this stuff is the stuff of legend. All the details are suspect. Because there is so little you know, your mind is free to fill in the gaps with whatever you want. Create your own boogeyman, it can literally be anybody. All those little details, they can all change, because the truth of the legend is what's important.

It's said there was this guy who decided one day he was sick and tired of the cops harassing him. He really wanted to show em, to get em good. He decided to plant a booby trap. It would work for sure, there was no way it would fail. They could fuck with him all they wanted, but he was gonna get his.

So he sets his trap, gets the ball rolling, then commits his crime. Maybe he robs someone – scratch that, he probably punches someone in the face or better yet, he breaks into a car. He's not trying to hurt anyone who doesn't deserve it. Burglary from a motor vehicle is a property crime. A felony, so it's serious enough to draw a legit response, but it's not rob someone serious. Worst case, he'll get time served or spend a couple months in jail, but more likely than not, he'll just get probation.

Point is, it's gotta be fairly low consequence. Because the real star of the show is the trap. He doesn't think there's even a penal code for this one.

So instead of fleeing the scene, he sticks around. He dares someone to call the cops. He begs them to call the cops. Because this guy's a certain brand of crazy. Plan's already in motion.

When the cops show up, he throws a courtesy "Fuck you!" their way. He gets a little mouthy, just to sell it, but overall he's going with the program. He doesn't want to get tased or anything. He really plays up the whole drunken ass- hole thing to make it seem real. It is real, but not in how they're expecting.

Once they get him in the cuffs, it's all standard proce- dure. He's been through it before. He knows they're gonna pat him down for weapons and then empty his pockets into a property bag. You do this because you don't want the guy leaving any surprises for you in the backseat – surprises like syringes, crack pipes, other contraband. You always search him first before putting him in your car.

The one copper pats him down, checks his waistband for weapons, all while his partner grabs a property bag from the trunk. While the partner holds the bag open, the other guy reaches into his pockets to remove the property. He pulls out a wallet, some old wrappers, a crumpled receipt, some loose change. He reaches into the other pocket ex- pecting to find something similar. Except it's different. It's really different.

He reaches in somewhat slowly, just to be careful, be- cause he knows guys out there tend to carry "sharps," or needles. You have to go a little slower because you don't want to get stuck. He even asks him before he reaches in, "You have anything in your pockets that are gonna poke me?"

The guy answers no.

He even asks him again, just to really emphasize how serious he is, "You sure?"

The guy re-affirms, says he doesn't have anything sharp in there. But he does say he has an old pipe. The cop reaches in expecting to find something that feels like a small, narrow glass cylinder.

Except it's not.

He pulls his hand out. And immediately he knows what it is.

He just grabbed a handful of shit. A handful of human shit. Feces. Straight up doo doo, chock full of nuggets and tidbits and moist and stinky.

And our criminal, he bursts out laughing. Best prank he's ever pulled. It'd even be worth the time in the unlikely chance that he would even get any, just to have seen the look on this cop's face one more time, once he realized what he was grabbing.

"It's mine, motherfucker!"

And that's the story. That's the legend. The details don't matter, because the truth is that there exists out there a man, who may be either black or white or Hispanic or Asian, who may be tall or short or skinny or fat, who may be drunk or on drugs or even stone cold sober, who once planted a handful of his own shit in his coat pocket and then committed a crime, intending full well on getting caught. And he did it all out of spite, specifically knowing that the arresting officer would reach his hand into his pocket to grab an awful surprise. And because the mind is free to fill in the details, to cover all those gaps, the scary thing is it could literally be anybody. Might be the guy sitting in your back seat. It might be the guy breaking into a car at the call you're currently driving to.

Training officers tell their rookies this story. Why? Because it teaches a very valuable lesson, which is to always glove up before you search someone's pockets. For some reason, the prospect of grabbing a handful of human shit is far scarier than getting poked with an errant syringe. The idea of catching HIV from a sharp may be scary in concept, but most people don't have any true idea of what that actually means. You can't see it, it's an invisible killer, it's nebulous. But a handful of shit? Different story.

And when rookies ask why the hell anyone would do something like that, the only real response anyone can give as to the reason, is that he thought it would be funny. And boy did that guy laugh.

Regular Things and Weird Things and Harmonious Things

There's always a twist.

It may not always seem like a twist, but at a minimum, there's most definitely always an element of randomness when it comes to the streets. Sometimes you can see it coming down the road right at you, sudden as it may be – think Jimmy and the van. It may *seem* random, and it most definitely catches you at least somewhat by surprise, but on some level you sort of expect it.

It's one of those things you can ponder and break down by about five or six layers. For the Jimmy caper, consider all the steps I'd taken to get to that point. I *knew* I was going to be getting into a potentially dangerous career field when I became a cop in the first place, and I *knew* it was going to be amplified by that much more when I decided to do so in Los Angeles, and I *knew* it was going to be at a higher ridiculousness factor when I requested to be assigned to Central, and I *knew* I would be immersed in it when I was initially voluntold and then later volunteered to work Skid Row, and ultimately I *knew* the risk of running into something like that would be that much higher while doing laps at 2am.

I knew all of this leading up to it, so on some level I certainly must have been expecting it, or subconsciously maybe was even hoping for it. In a sense, something like that is an expected surprise.

Then there are other times when things just happen so simply and perfectly, where there are zero surprises or twists. Those end up having a surreal quality of their own, when there isn't some crazy angle. And in those cases, the perfect normalcy of it ends up being the twist.

There are guys like Abhijeet Absalom. Only reason I remember his name is because it was so unique. We stopped him on San Pedro St. south of 6th St, west side of the street next to the Midnight Mission. He was drinking a 211 malt liquor, the street beverage of choice. Has an aftertaste that really puts you in the mood to rob someone – 211 PC happens to be the penal code for robbery, for which the drink is named after.

Sabrina and I jammed him, it was an easy enough stop, nothing particularly noteworthy. Abhijeet was no different than dozens of guys we'd stopped for similar violations. He wasn't exactly nice, but he wasn't a complete asshole to us either. He was a big guy, taller than most, around 602, 240 pounds, and he had dreads. Turns out his name was about the most interesting thing about that interaction. You don't run into too many Abhijeet's in downtown LA. To this day, he's the only Abhijeet I've ever met, and I've met a lot of people.

We ran him, didn't find anything too outrageous, made some idle small talk, and gave him a warning for the beverage. We asked him to pour it out in exchange for not getting a citation. He obliged us, thankful we weren't going to give him a ticket. Easy stop, one for the books, it's good to be productive. Weird that it went so smoothly.

Stories like that seem simple, they seem so ordinary. And objectively, they are. It's a true one-off. You didn't know the guy, he did something he wasn't supposed to do, you stopped him, gave him a warning or maybe a ticket, and that was the end of it. Most police interactions tend to be viewed in this type of context, and so most policies tend to be crafted with this being the expectation.

Take something like a body worn video camera policy. The policy may state that for every public interaction, the camera needs to be activated as soon as possible to document the encounter. Think a ped stop like Abhijeet's, or a motorcycle cop stopping a speeder. The reason for the stop is simple – violation observed, enforcement action taken, and it's all documented. Easy to parse into a policy, easy to establish the objectivity. No surprises, no twists.

But reality rarely plays that way. A lot of cops complain about it, and similarly, a lot of folks simply don't grasp the element of randomness in which the world seems to operate. Both sides come at it from the extreme perspectives – one side says there's no reason they should have to worry about activating a camera and it's not fair because of all the "what-ifs" and "gotcha" opportunities for the bureaucracy to burn them on if they happen to mess up.

"What if I don't activate my camera in time, I'm worried about fighting this guy who randomly charged me while I was eating a burrito!"

But how often does that really happen? Certainly, sense and reason have to factor into it at least *somehow*. The response to something like that is, "Well maybe you should activate your camera for your whole shift." Which of course is not realistic either, and suddenly we're back to that whole sense and reason discussion. Reality isn't predictable and reality isn't pretty – of course, except when it is.

Remember, there's always a twist.

Not to mention, a camera can't capture everything, not with all the randomness, not with all the bizarreness that plays out in all its absurdity. It can't capture when you knew a guy from a previous encounter and how you expected him to react based on that prior knowledge, and just as much so, it can't capture things that were about to happen. A camera can't capture how tired you are circling a neighborhood at 2am. It can't capture how uncomfortable you are while a perv sings a song while sitting next to you in the back of your car. A camera can't capture a person's state of mind. A camera can't capture fear or adrenaline or suspicion or compassion or shame or desperation or a number of other emotional drivers that move people to do the things they do, on either side of the law.

That's why an interaction like Abhijeet's, an interaction that goes so smoothly, that goes so by the book, starts to feel surreal on some level. No curveballs, no special circumstances. Nothing weird or uncomfortable or unusual. Just simple. Basic. And you grow suspicious, because instinctively you've been conditioned to expect the surprises, all these other elements that come along with it. You come to expect the strange angle, to expect it all to somehow spin in some wildly unpredictable manner.

What's the spin here? What's it gonna be? Still looking for that twist...

Later that evening, Sabrina and I are on another call. Some frat guys who live in one of the lofts at 6th and San Pedro are filming a movie – a small budget student type film, in the lobby of their building. They've got some lights, a few crew members, somebody's operating a boom mic, a small table off to the side with water bottles and snacks. Somebody passing by had seen them and called the police, claiming there was a robbery in progress. I guess one of the scenes they were shooting involved a fist fight, so as the actors were throwing blows, somebody decided it looked real enough to call it in. Never mind the obvious film crew.

Of course, we get there and get to chatting with these kids. They're all kinds of shook, getting jammed by the cops, but it's really not a big deal. We're not gonna bust their balls for not having permits, they're film students, probably doing it for a class. I used to produce student films in college, so I know that permits and all that aren't really much of a consideration for ultra-low budget projects like most student short films. They're excited to hear I actually went to film school back in the day, curious to know how I managed to become a cop in LA. It's nice to talk with someone who isn't a crackhead every now and then, a refreshing change of pace.

Out of the corner of my eye I see somebody stumbling towards us. Sabrina notices too. Probably a drunk. She turns to address him while I'm chatting with the kids, when she calls me away suddenly.

"Partner, this guy's bleeding, I'm gonna get him an ambulance."

"What happened?"

"He says he got hit in the head, that he got robbed over by San Julian."

Somebody got robbed on San Julian. You don't say?

I tell the kids to maybe have a couple crew members stand outside with a sign, or maybe have them post up so it's a little more obvious they're making a student film. They thank me and agree to take some extra precautions.

I make my way back over to Sabrina and the old man. He's sitting on the sidewalk now, thankful to be off his feet. Ambulance is on its way. He's an older Armenian guy, and he's bleeding from his face, has a big cut on the side of his head, ripped and torn shirt and pants, looks like he got worked over pretty good.

Sabrina asks him, "You said you got robbed, what happened exactly?"

"I need an ambulance!" he yells.

"The ambulance is coming, you need to tell me what happened so we can let the other officers know who to go look for on the radio."

The guy mumbles to himself for a bit, trying to find the words. He stammers, "I don't know, I don't know. I was walking by the park around the corner, and all of a sudden somebody came up from behind me and threw a big blanket over my head and started beating me. And I fell down and they kept hitting me, and then they took my briefcase, it had my watches in it."

"Watches?"

"Yes, I work at the jewelry store on Broadway, I was going there."

"Was it just one guy, or could you tell if it was more than one?" Sabrina asks.

"I think it was more than one, they had different voices."

Our guy continues moaning and complaining, so we assure him the ambulance is nearby. We can't fault the man, he's legit hurt. He starts bleeding more. Hopefully he doesn't pass out.

Within a few minutes, the ambulance pulls up and Sabrina updates them on the situation while I scratch down what I can of the guy's info for the robbery report.

He's obviously having a shitty day, so we don't tell him to his face, but we're a little suspicious. Is this guy legit? Yeah, he definitely got worked over and that's not right, but what did *he* do? He had to have been trying to score some rock. I bet if we ran his rap, he'd have arrests for possession. What was he doing walking down 5th, why was he near San Julian? That's the most dangerous street in LA. If he truly works at the shop on Broadway, then he's gotta be familiar with the area. He has to know better than to walk down that street, not with something as obviously attractive to a criminal looking to make a quick score as a goddamn briefcase, of all things. We've seen out of towners accidentally pass through and get hemmed up, but this guy? At 10pm? No way, I'm not buying it. What's the twist?

There's not much to put out in terms of a crime broadcast. What would I even say, robbery suspect last seen near San Julian Park, may be armed with a blanket? Nice broadcast Chris, really gave the other cops working the area something to go on, that's gonna solve the case for sure.

No, we decide after we get the guy on his way to head back to the office to check the cameras, maybe they captured the assault. We have a rough timestamp of when it happened, so we can maybe search within a thirty-minute window near where he described. San Julian is a fairly small park, we're sure to have cameras covering most of the street he was probably walking on.

We start reviewing and low and behold, just like he described, he's walking down 5th St. right near the park when two guys randomly come up behind him. Out of nowhere, just happens. One guy takes a giant blanket and throws it over his head, and the two of them begin beating him senseless – throwing kicks, punches, along his whole body and head. It's a brutal attack. Wow, this guy was telling the truth. Jaded cops that we were thought he was probably loitering in the area trying to score dope and got jumped, said the wrong thing to the wrong person. But nope – he was telling the truth. An actual victim, strange when that happens.

We start breaking down the video, noting the times, the details, trying to get a closer look at the assailants. We think we recognize one of them. I start to ask, "Is that –

"That's Fat Freddy!" Sabrina exclaims.

"That *is* Fat Freddy, that fat motherfucker! That's him, isn't it!"

Fat Freddy is one of the local Grape Street gangsters, a real dickhead. Neighborhood bully, a troublemaker. Fat too. His game is usually dope sales – he hangs out around San Julian Park and deals rock, but he's also been known to do quite a few strong-arm robberies.

He was one of the guys who would jump people near this dark alcove outside the local market after they'd use the ATM. That was another big problem we always had, on the fifteenth and the thirtieth of every month. As soon as everyone's government checks would come in and their debit cards would get reloaded, the first thing they would do would be to hit the local ATM to take out some cash, usually to buy dope. Drug dealers typically don't accept credit cards, go figure. And as soon as they'd pull out the money, somebody would be waiting right there nearby to mug them.

Freddy was one of these guys, even though we could never officially pin it on him. People would describe him, and we would know who they were talking about, but being the nature of Skid Row, it's rare to find an actual cooperative victim, much less a coherent one who could accurately ID a suspect. So Fat Freddy had been skating by.

We knew he was on parole for an old sales case, but who out there wasn't? That was always enough to jam him, but lotta good that was gonna do if we didn't have a crime we could charge him with. Not until now. Because there he was on video, recognizable, throwing a blanket over some old man's head and putting a beating on him and snatching his briefcase. That's the kind of evidence that plays really well in court.

Then there's the other guy. We look a little closer, and suddenly both Sabrina and I look at each other, like we finally figured out the last piece to the puzzle, like we just solved the Da Vinci Code.

Together, we both say his name, "Abhijeet!"

From earlier. The smooth, simple interaction that appeared not to have any greater significance. We knew there had to be a twist. There's almost always a twist.

There he was, the same guy we stopped earlier for drinking a 211, now committing a 211 clear as day. Not only did we clearly have him on video when we stopped him earlier, but now we also had him on video wearing the exact same outfit, going to town on this poor old man with Fat Freddy. We didn't know the two of them knew each other.

I send out a group message to our guys who are still in the field, letting them know that Fat Freddy is good to go on a 211 if they see him out there. Same with Abhijeet Absalom, if they happened to know who he was. Had em both on video, caught red-handed.

It wasn't before long that another unit spotted Fat Freddy, hanging out by the ATM outside the corner store, of all places. They gave us a call and told us to meet. We showed up and the four of us jammed him, brought him back to the station without any issues.

The key is you don't tell him right off the bat what he's being taken for – you gotta soft sell it to him so he doesn't try to run or fight you. Conversation goes something like this, we tell him, "Hey Freddy, we gotta bring you in to the station."

"Why, what I do this time?!"

"Man, we got a couple wits said they saw you involved in some kind of fight earlier. You know anything about that?

"Naa man, that's not how I do, you know my game."

"Yeah I know, but that's what they're saying."

"I really gotta go wit' you guys?"

"Yeah bro, I'll show you what we got when we get back. Have I ever lied to you?"

Freddy shakes his head and walks forward, defeated-like. He turns around willingly, I put him in cuffs, and help him into the backseat of the car. One suspect down, one still outstanding.

*   *   *

We found Abhijeet the next day. It was me, Bermudez, and Phil – we were riding three deep. Before we went out, I gave them a rundown of the caper from the night before, ran them through how Sabrina and I got flagged down by the old guy, saw what happened on the security footage, saw how Fat Freddy and Abhijeet threw the blanket over him and beat him, and then how we finally jammed Fat Freddy like an hour later.

Phil asked me, "Nice, so you guys got him, what'd he say?"

Turns out, Fat Freddy was a liar. We brought him in and made our way back to detectives. There is an interrogation room in the back. We walk him in there and have him sit down across the table from us.

"You're not gonna freak out or fight or anything if I take the cuffs off, right?"

"Naa homie, I'm good."

"Ok, lean forward." I walk behind Freddy and remove the handcuffs as he's seated at the table. He pulls his arms out and stretches. The cuffs aren't designed for comfort.

Fat Freddy is a black kid, about twenty-five years old, about 511 and heavyset, easily 250 pounds. He's got messy cornrows, or at least bunches that used to be cornrows, but he hasn't been keeping up with them. He's all kinds of shoddy looking. He's wearing a grey wife-beater tank top with too many holes in it, dirty black sweat shorts, black sneakers with white tube socks, and he has a dirty white bandage wrapped around his right arm by the elbow. He's not making any effort to hide how slovenly he actually looks – he's just sort of embracing it. It makes his fatness that much more of a character trait, really adds to his coming off as that much more of a hot mess. It's baffling because he actually has a place to stay down in Watts, but he prefers to hang out on Skid Row, it's just his thing.

I start, "So what happened earlier?"

"What you mean, what happened earlier?"

Freddy looks at me with a confused look, but it's obvious he's not confused. He's very calculating. But like Armando, he isn't a good enough actor to pull off a convincing fake.

"Come on bro, you know what this is all about."

"I swear, dead homies, I don't know what you talkin' about."

"Dead homies?"

"Yeah, dead homies bro, I'm serious."

"I never heard dead homies before, is that new?"

"Naa bro, you know me, I'm minding my own business tonight."

I purse my lips and cock my head slightly, trying to convey without having to say the words, really?

And Freddy is just sitting there with a dumb look on his face, the kind of look that says, ask me more questions so I

can obviously lie to you and pretend I'm telling the truth, even though we both know I'm not fooling anybody.

I continue the conversation, "About an hour ago, ehh, maybe ninety minutes by now, there was a fight of some sort over by 5th and San Julian, just outside the park. Where were you?"

Freddy responds, "I was hanging out at the Rescue."

"Now remember, we got people saying they saw you there."

"An hour ago? Man, I was in the stairwell behind the Union Rescue, me and my boy were smoking, we was just chillin'."

"Freddy, don't lie to us. You don't even smell like anything, your eyes aren't even red."

Sabrina chimes in, "They're not bloodshot or anything. Come on."

"I'm high as hell right now bro, you don't even know!"

I shake my head, "Freddy, I know you're not high, I've seen you high. And if you're claiming you're high and we book you for robbery, you know you're gonna get stuck in medical all damn night."

"Robbery?! I didn't rob nobody, dead homies!"

"Dead homies?"

"Dead homies, I didn't rob nobody! You know what I do, I don't rob nobody, I only sell, you know what I do."

"I'm gonna show you something, you sure you don't want to change your story, that you were getting high in the stairwell?"

"Dead homies."

Sabrina hands me her cell phone with the video already cued up. I play the video for him and we can both see, clear as day, Freddy with the blanket, throwing it over the old man. Then the whirlwind assault.

"Ok that's not what it looks like!"

Sabrina blurts out, "Hah!"

"I swear, I didn't rob him!"

Baffled, I say, "Freddy, I just watched you watch a video of yourself beating the shit out of the man and robbing him, and you say it's not what it looks like?!"

"I didn't rob him, I only assaulted him! That's just a battery!"

Sabrina and I exchange a quick glance. Is he really trying to school us on the penal code?

"The man had to go to the hospital!"

"But I didn't rob him, I know what robbery is and I didn't rob him."

"You stole his briefcase!"

Freddy shakes his head and points back at the cell phone, "No I didn't, watch it again, it was the other guy who stole his briefcase. All I did was a battery, that's a misdemeanor only, ain't no felony robbery!"

All the gangsters know the penal codes, state certified street lawyers.

I continue, dismissing his reasoning, "Even so, guy got beat up and his things got taken. By the looks of this video, it seems like you two were working together."

"Santiago, look at me, fuck that, I don't even know that guy, dead homies!"

"So the two of you just happened to beat the shit out of this guy at the same time and then stopped beating him at the same time and then ran off in the same direction. Also at the same time. Whose idea was it?"

Freddy retorts, sticking to his guns, "I don't even know him, I hit him because I saw him earlier and he was talking shit, just putting him in his place, dead homies, you know how it works out there."

"What about the other guy, just decided to jump in and help for no reason?"

"He must have, saw me hitting him and decided to jump in and get his."

I shake my head, "Freddy, you know this is really hard to believe that you two weren't working together."

"I swear, you know my game, I only sell, I don't rob people." Except that he does.

"But you admit that you assaulted him."

"That's a misdemeanor, I didn't rob him."

"If you say so, Freddy."

"I swear I didn't rob him, dead homies!"

We talk a little more, he may or may not know the guy. Just as likely that he doesn't know him, but it doesn't really matter. Even if he didn't intend to rob him, it was all a part of the same fluid incident. The overarching crime was robbery, and Freddy was most definitely one of the key players to that end. In addition to him being recognizable in the video and the fact that he was wearing the same outfit and the same bandage when he got jammed as when he committed the crime, by his own words, he placed himself at the scene and admitted to the violent assault. More than enough to charge him for the robbery.

"You know you're gonna have to get booked for the robbery, right?"

Resigned, Freddy lowers his head, as if ashamed. Not at what he did, but at the fact that he got caught. "Yeah, I know."

"You still claiming you're high, or do you wanna skip medical?"

Freddy laughs, "You know I ain't high, Santiago!"

The whole point of the interrogation was to see if he would implicate Abhijeet, which he either couldn't or wouldn't do. In any case, we'd have to try to get Abhijeet to implicate himself in the off chance we actually tracked him down. Even though we had the video, there was always the possibility that the defense might say it was too grainy or otherwise unusable for one reason or another. Always better to have more corroborating evidence than less, and statements made by the defendant under Miranda always play the best.

I finish pitching the previous night's caper to Phil and Bermudez, and Phil asks, "Why did he keep saying dead homies?"

"I don't know, never heard it before. Bermudez, you ever hear anybody say that?"

"Nope, I never heard that. Must be new."

We pack up our gear, load into the car and make our way out into the world.

We're out there cruising around for maybe thirty minutes when Bermudez comes through. Bermudez, the street cop superman, able to spot the one guy we're looking for in a sea of hundreds of faces, just like that.

It's a goddamn mystery how he's able to do it. He'd never even seen, let alone met Abhijeet before, but he spotted him only a block away from where Sabrina and I jammed him the previous day. And what was he doing, you might ask? Drinking another 211.

I'd call it serendipitous, but I don't even know if that's the word that really describes it. It's more an uncanny sense of harmony, of it all working out too goddamn perfectly, to the point that it draws suspicion. At least in our minds. We couldn't have written it more unbelievably – the one guy we were looking for, first thing out, within thirty minutes. Only way it was possible was because of Bermudez, it's surreal.

To say Bermudez is talented or has a unique skill is an understatement. It really does border along magical. If a little falsetto rang out every time Bermudez spotted somebody who was wanted, we could conduct a whole opera over the course of a month. If an angel got its wings every time Bermudez spotted a warrant suspect, the wings would be on backorder from heaven. To watch him work is sublime.

Rumor has it, he once recognized a guy by his feet. His *feet*. He was doing a foot patrol – no pun intended – with some other cops near 6th and Towne one night, and the four of them started talking to a couple of locals. Just a casual encounter, no enforcement, just making the rounds. Bermudez keeps walking, wanders away by about twenty paces or so from the other three, and he stops and looks down at somebody sleeping on the ground. This guy's just lying there, head tucked away in a partially opened tent, covered by a couple blankets, and with a few empty beer cans littered next to his sleeping heap on the floor.

Bermudez waves them over, "Guys, this is Ricky. He's got a warrant."

The three coppers walk over to him and ask him, "Ricky?"

"I forget his last name, but he's got a new warrant out. That's him. I have his file over in my bag."

"Dude, all you can see are his feet, are you sure?"

"That's him alright."

They wake the guy up, ask for an ID, and low and behold, it's Ricky. Legendary.

Bermudez spots Abhijeet, and both Phil and I take a glance. We can't tell, but if Bermudez is saying it's him, it must be him. I flip the car around and pull up on the small group. We tell Abhijeet to come over towards us and for everyone else to give us some space. We handcuff him easily enough and put him in the car.

Of course, everyone else is pissed off, saying we're kidnapping him this and that, but they haven't seen the video. I explain why he's being placed under arrest, that he was identified as having taken part in a robbery the night before, and let them know where we're taking him. If they're that concerned, they can always post his bail. I get in the car and off we go back to the station.

Processing is easy, paperwork is coming along. There're no shenanigans going on in the back tank. It's all going so smoothly. There's gotta be something wrong. Things don't just *go* this smoothly.

And no sooner than I'm thinking about it, it finally starts to happen. Abhijeet starts sweating. And not just sweating because he's a little uncomfortable or a little nervous – he looks like he's just run a 5k. He's sweating profusely, dripping. And he's far more agitated. He's getting angrier and angrier. People walking by are giving *us* dirty looks, like what kind of maniac did we bring in…and there *wasn't* a use of force?

We have him handcuffed to the bench in the report writing room. He starts demanding we let him take off his shirt, but we're not going to do that. He starts cursing, then demanding even further, then he's yelling, then he's cursing some more, then he's trying to stand up and rip the bench from its bolts. He's straining and flexing his muscles so hard the handcuffs are digging into his wrists, and we can see the blood starting to find its way out.

Little did we know, Abhijeet had just taken a hit of PCP only moments before we jammed him. PCP is a drug that's way crazier than crack or meth. It's sold in a vial and comes as a clear yellowish liquid. Users will usually take a cigarette and dip one end in the liquid, then light the cigarette and smoke it. The effects of PCP take a little bit to get into your system, but when you start to feel the effects, you really start to *feel* the effects. You start sweating, you become incredibly irritable, and you get really hot. And angry.

People who are high on PCP almost always strip their clothes off, and they will walk down the street buck ass naked, smashing anything and everything in their path. Cars, fences, trash cans, other people, you name it. And all with a swinging dick hitting everything in sight.

And much like the Hulk, when you're high on PCP, you get super human strength combined with a ridiculously high pain tolerance. Tasers don't take people down who are on PCP. Pepper spray won't do the trick. You've seen the Rodney King video – things get ugly.

The human body is a dynamic and powerful machine. There are stories of moms, average sized women, lifting cars to save their children. They're fueled by nothing more than pure adrenaline and maternal drive. The only thing that keeps people from tapping into it all the time is the body's natural ability to regulate for the sake of self-preservation.

Sure, you can push your body to the extreme, but it may break. PCP turns that regulator off. That's why it will usually take anywhere from ten to fifteen cops to try and arrest someone who's on a PCP fueled bender. You can look up the videos, they're wild.

Lucky for us, Abhijeet isn't strong enough to defeat the handcuffs or the steel bench, so he rages while he remains chained to it. There's no way we're going to transport him ourselves, so we call an ambulance for the transport. He's obviously under some kind of medical duress, being under the influence and whatnot.

Our plan is for them to show up and have them help us strap him to the gurney using the leather restraints, and they'll haul him off to the hospital where he can be sedated for awhile.

As I'm signing him out, the watch commander looks at me while shaking his head. "You guys and your unit, never fails."

"Robbery suspect off the streets, what can we say."

I raise my eyebrows and shake my head. I sign him out and then head back out to the car. Unbelievable. Why couldn't he have been chill, like Freddy? Because he started freaking out, we never even got a chance to interview him. Hopefully the case holds up. I knew this wouldn't be easy.

And it doesn't get easier. While at the hospital in the jail ward, Abhijeet is so fired up that the doctor has to give him a double dose of the cocktail, and he's raging so much that he actually breaks two hospital beds.

The jailers strap him down with even more leather straps. It takes some time before the cocktail works its way into his system before he finally settles.

You hate to think otherwise, because you do your best to view the people you interact with as human. This is, after all, a person who has, or at least at some point, had a family, had a life. It may not be their fault they're slumming it on Skid Row. It may not be their fault the world rejected them, or that they fell off the right track and got mixed up with the wrong crowd. Sometimes people just get lost in the shit.

But at some point, you have to take stock and try to reconcile the differences between what you know to be intellectually and morally the right way to frame the world, and the way it manifests right in front of you. When those inherent rules are constantly being violated by what you see and witness, it becomes increasingly difficult to maintain that grounded view.

It's a real conundrum, when a situation *feels* different than how you *know* it should be. It's the mark of true absurdity. How do you view someone who is acting like a raging animal as anything but? It's a perverse challenge of the mind, and you have to commit to fighting that impulse. It requires constant reflection to keep it from becoming the default.

It's when you lose that perspective, when that becomes the standard, that you know you've been there too long. At that point, *you're* the one who's been institutionalized. That's the twist you're trying to avoid.

*   *   *

After getting his dose, Abhijeet finally passed out. That gave Bermudez time to go absentee book him at the jail while Phil and I babysat the body. Not having to worry about managing your arrestee makes the admin part a lot less stressful – it's just paperwork, nothing to deal with other than maybe a slow computer.

Abhijeet finally came to some hours later. When you factor in the recovery time and the fact that the hospital had to monitor him before just sending us on our way, it easily turned into an all-night caper. Like I said before, it can be a quick ten-minute thing or it can be an all-night fiasco. Just another day downtown.

After coming down from such a high, when the energy level drops, it doesn't quite go away. It just reconfigures itself into a kind of nervous tension. Everything's smooth and easy again, just like before. But you never actually relax. In the back of your mind you know, you fear, that it will all spiral again so suddenly. You're not scared of the danger itself; you're scared of the chaos and stress that comes with it. You're scared of the paperwork and the logistics of managing a crisis that will put you over hours and hours when you're tired and worn out. So you keep your guard up. Physically, mentally, and emotionally. Can't get caught slipping.

As we make our way into the jail, past the drunks and thieves and all the same people who always seem to be in there, and past the female jailer and past the check-in station and back to medical, it all reeks of that same sense of unease. Like you're one wrong word away from an incident, one mistake away from a crisis, from it all unraveling. Like boot camp. That sick feeling from the anticipation creeps in, when you're expecting it but it never comes, the calm before the storm.

Abhijeet sits on the plastic chairs outside medical. Phil and I wait with him while Bermudez makes his way into the nurse's station. He hands her his medical "Cleared to Book" paperwork from the hospital.

We made sure to send in Bermudez to get the blessing from medical – he's always bringing in the worst bodies so they all know him. Because he's the one usually bringing them in, he's developed the best rapport with the staff. Any other medical obstacles and they might fix it for us on the back end just because we're working with him, as opposed to sending us to some other facility and prolonging our night.

Even though Abhijeet's been through medical at the hospital already, we can't just drop him off at the jail and leave. The medical staff still need to review his file so they know who will be in their care. So we wait. We wait and we wait while they review and decide, and the tension keeps building.

"Next!"

We stand up Abhijeet and walk him back to see the doctor. He sits down on a soft blue vinyl covered chair, the kind you find in most doctors' offices. He's still cuffed behind his back.

The nurse asks, "Can we take his cuffs off?"

The three of us get really wide eyed and shake our heads no. She gets the hint.

She takes his blood pressure, listens to his breathing, gets his heart rate, asks him if he's feeling any pain or needs anything from them and he says no. He thanks them. Suddenly he's very polite.

The doc reviews his file, signs off on it, and hands us his paperwork and sends us on our way, over to the drop off window.

We're walking past those same people again. One step down, one step closer to being done. I can almost feel the warmth of my bed, I imagine how refreshing a nice hot shower will be after such a long day dealing with this sweaty, angry fellow. But we're not home free, not just yet. Can't let those thoughts distract, need to stay focused, need to see it through. Don't let it spiral, you've managed the chaos so far.

Drop off window, last step of the booking process.

It doesn't even cross our minds that we haven't eaten all day. We got stuck with this one pretty much right out the gate and have been constantly on the go. At least this one wasn't a masturbation caper – this was at least a robbery. We'd be closing the file on a legit case. That always makes it a little easier to bear, the hassle of going through the motions and dealing with the difficulty of the process, knowing it's at least a serious matter and not just bizarre for the sake of being bizarre.

Then there's another twist.

Abhijeet turns to me and politely asks, "Good sir, would you kindly remove me from these hand shackles?"

He says it in a British accent.

"Excuse me?"

"I do require your assistance, if you would be so kind as to remove me from these shackles, such that I may abscond from this horrid, wretched prison. My benefactors will surely see you compensated for your troubles."

Something's not right. Is he doing a bit? Like Shakespeare?

"I can't take them off yet, we gotta finish booking you and then the jailers can take the cuffs off."

"But sir! I do require their removal if I am to leave this filthy dungeon! Oh, have I suffered so within these walls, tormented in this dankness, all the troubled minds and wretched souls alike, suffering, crying out for freedom!"

Shakespeare wrote a lot of stories, but I don't think he ever wrote anything about a PCP fueled rage machine doing a soliloquy in a jail. Unless I'm really mis-remembering Othello...

"Sorry man, can't take em off yet."

Abhijeet looks defeated. His dreads dangle over his eyes, his clothes bathed in the musky stench of the streets, an odor mixed with drugs and alcohol laced sweat and of course, the unmistakable stench of feces. It always smells like feces. He's definitely shit himself during some point of this whole ordeal. He raises his head triumphantly.

"Sir!"

"Yes?"

"Sir! Then oblige me this, I have but one request, on good conscience, on the blood and honor of my ancestors! That I here challenge you to a duel! Remove me from these shackles and you shall choose the weapons! If you defeat me, I will remand myself into thy custody and be taken to my cell, to forever remain imprisoned, alone and forever shamed, stripped of my honor. But if I win –

"Yes?"

"Sir! I say, Sir! If I win! Then and only then, you shall declare to the magistrate that I be set free, and I shall breathe a new breath of freedom! What say you?!"

Phil and Bermudez are just staring, wide eyed. A couple other officers who were walking by, now they've stopped. He's attracting a crowd. And he just challenged me to a duel.

It doesn't matter if you're doing Shakespeare or Tupac, whether you're on the streets of Paris in 17th century France or on the streets of Skid Row in 2017. If someone challenges you to a duel, you can't just ignore it. The streets won't let you. You either step up or you step down, unless you can somehow manage to outwit the challenger and save face. But even Alexander Hamilton couldn't pull that off.

I decide to lean into it and embrace the crazy.

"My good gentleman," I say as I lower my voice, "It is regrettable that I cannot accept your challenge at the present time. But if we must duel, and duel we must – then the weapon I choose to wield, and I shall wield it with the force of a thousand swords, shall be the law, I say! I wield the law! And I shall see you at dawn on the third day, bright and early at your arraignment!"

I hand the last of the papers to the clerk, and a couple jailers make their way around and take Abhijeet by the arms. They escort him to a cell, remove the cuffs, and usher him inside. They close the door and head back towards me. As they hand me my handcuffs, "Central or Hollywood?"

"Central."

As I'm walking away, I hear Abhijeet calling out to me from his cell, "But sir! Please sir! Sir! Listen to me, I beg of you! Sir!"

He never let up with the accent.

Some people just can't accept reality. But then again, if you were Abhijeet, why would you want to?

The other officers who were watching the performance have already moved on. Nothing else to see here, just another thing.

Phil and Bermudez laugh while we start heading out. I stop in the booking office to grab an extra pair of gloves and to wash my hands.

It's been a long day, thankfully we're done. Hot shower's waiting at home. Subpoena will probably come through in about a week when they file the charges, nice to have worked a case from beginning to end like this, strange as it was. It was ordinary and weird and harmonious, all at the same time. Classic Central caper.

And as I'm leaving, walking past the crackheads and thieves and gangsters and pervs, I suddenly notice something that was only faint before. A steady beat that's been playing in the background for the last few minutes. A familiar beat.

I pause and step backwards towards the front office. The radio's on and somebody's listening to a song. It's the eighties station. It's a special song that holds a dear place in my heart, a song that brings back feelings and emotions and smells and images and sensations and all the rest of the parts that make up your memories, the truest elements of your stories. And the watch commander is sitting in the office, bobbing his head along.

Tainted love, whooaa…

Fucking Soft Cell.